GOING
BACK
TO
SCHOOL

Frank J. Bruno, Ph.D.

Macmillan • USA

Second Edition

Copyright © 1998, 1995 by Frank J. Bruno, Ph.D.

Macmillan General Reference USA
A Simon & Schuster Macmillan Company
1633 Broadway
New York, NY 10019-6785

An Arco Book

Manufactured in the United States of America

10 9 8 7 6 5 4 3 2 1

Library of Congress Number: 97-81088
ISBN: 0-02-862514-5

To those with unfulfilled academic dreams
and vocational goals

ACKNOWLEDGMENTS

A number of people have helped me make *Going Back to School* a reality. My thanks are expressed to:

Barabara Gilson, Senior Editor at Macmillan, for her recognition of the value of the book and for being a supportive and creative editor.

Bert Holtje, my agent, for encouraging the development of the book.

Robert Segui, Matriculation Counselor at San Bernardino Valley College, for providing information pertaining to study skills and academic success.

Kathleen Flynn, Re-entry Coordinator at San Bernardino Valley College, for providing information pertaining to the concept of the nontraditional student.

My wife, Jeanne, for our many meaningful discussions about the educational process.

My son, Franklin, for our conversations about teaching and learning.

George K. Zaharoupoulos, a true teaching colleague, for his steadfast encouragement of my writing projects.

CONTENTS

PREFACE

One of Your Best Friends in College

Going Back to School could become one of your best friends in college. How can a book be a friend? A book is more than a thing—it is a mind. Specifically, this book represents my mind speaking to you, offering you advice, guidance, and practical suggestions based on many years of experience as both a student, a teacher, and a counseling psychologist.

This book represents more than just my mind at work. The ideas and useful findings of great thinkers and psychologists ranging from Aristotle to Sigmund Freud, from William James to B. F. Skinner, are also included. The book is unique in that it combines in one easy-to-use source a treasure chest of highly useful material gathered from educational psychology and learning theory. And it is all directed toward helping you, the adult in college.

This book can help you accomplish at least eleven things.

1. *Decide whether or not you belong in college.* Perhaps you have not yet enrolled in college, but you are thinking of going and you

have doubts about your ability. Chapter 1 dispels misconceptions about college and helps you make a decision that is right for you.

2. *See a pathway into college that will work for you.* Sometimes a college or university seems like a formidable castle with a moat and walls designed to defeat your best efforts and keep you out. Chapter 2 gives you general information about the nature of colleges and universities and removes much of the mystery surrounding them. Chapter 3 shows you how to gain admission to the college of your choice.

3. *Find practical ways to stay in college and succeed.* Many students drop out of college. Chapter 4 discusses the concept of the high-risk student, one who is vulnerable and likely to become discouraged. The chapter also presents a survey of student-support services designed to help you achieve your long-range academic goals.

4. *Develop self-confidence as an adult student.* Many adult students see themselves as inadequate and underprepared in comparison to other students. In the college setting they tend to adopt what the psychiatrist Eric Berne, author of *Games People Play*, called the "I'm not O.K.—You're O.K." life position. They think—incorrectly—that everyone else is more competent than they are. The many specific survival strategies outlined in this book will help you overcome any feelings of low self-esteem you have as a student.

5. *Discover effective ways to earn high grades.* Learning for the love of learning is important. It is an ideal held by many college professors, including me. Let's face it, however; the name of the game is *high grades*. There is a difference between learning itself and high grades. Learning is a *deep process* going on *within* the person. High grades are a measure of *performance*, and they may or may not be a good measure of real learning. In order to survive and accomplish your educational goals you *do* need to have ways to earn high grades. Fortunately, however, the methods are specific, and you will find them in this book. See Chapter 5 for an introduction to this subject.

6. *Cope with math anxiety.* A very common problem among adults in college is math anxiety. Your pulse races and your palms sweat when you think of taking a math class. Consequently, many students avoid such classes like the plague. And yet you may be required to take one or several math classes. You may even be tempted to drop out of college because of this requirement. Math

anxiety usually arises from experiences of failure in earlier grades and is related to a phenomenon known as *learned helplessness*. I know, because I suffered from math anxiety when I entered college. Chapters 8 and 13 will help you cope with math anxiety and learned helplessness.

7. *Cope with test anxiety.* Many students complain of general test anxiety. They say that their minds go blank or that they can't think clearly when they are taking a test. This kind of anxiety is really a *fear* of test taking, and it often interferes with performance. You can't demonstrate the learning that you actually have. (Note again the very real distinction between *learning* and *performance*.) Chapter 12 addresses itself to the problem of test anxiety and offers you practical ways to cope with it.

8. *Overcome feelings of doubt and defeat.* Feelings of doubt and defeat are just that—*feelings*. They are usually subjective magnifications of objective inadequacies and obstacles. Because they are subjective—they are within you and not in the real world—they can be overcome. Learned helplessness, referred to earlier, is a psychological process underlying the gloom-and-doom approach to a college career. Chapter 13 takes as its topic coping with learned helplessness and shows you how to replace it with a process called *learned optimism*. Overall, the material in the book will help you feel less unsure of yourself and more able to overcome both real and psychological barriers.

9. *Motivate yourself to do your best.* Lack of motivation is one of the principal reasons many students drop out of many classes, drop out of college completely, or turn in a poor academic performance. The *underachiever*, in high school or in college, is a person with ability but with little or no wind in his or her sails. What is required is a way of generating your own push, your own energy. The process of self-motivation should not be left completely to chance. There really *are* things that you can do for yourself in order to raise your spirits and get going. Chapter 7 pays particular attention to this highly important topic.

10. *Improve your memory.* In classical philosophy and early academic psychology, memory was looked upon as a faculty of the mind, a kind of inborn power. Some people had a powerful memory and others had a weak one, and not much could be done about it. Today this appears to be a fallacious viewpoint. Instead, contemporary psychology looks upon memory as a *process*. And if the process is breaking down at one of its stages, it can be corrected in

specific ways. You do need to have a properly functioning memory in order to succeed in college, and Chapter 14 shows you ways to develop an outstanding one.

11. *Realize your educational and vocational dreams.* This book takes a *can do* approach to higher education. It shows you in numerous ways exactly how you can become an effective, successful student. It also encourages you to maximize your talents and potentialities—a process the humanistic psychologist Abraham Maslow called *self-actualization.* This book can help you become the person you are meant to be.

In short, every chapter in the book is designed in some highly specific way to help you accomplish a definable goal that is associated with your survival and success as a college student.

As I said earlier, think of *Going Back to School* as one of your best friends in college. Refer to it often. I believe you will be glad that you selected it to become one of your close companions.

Above all, you will find the book *useful.* I wish you well.

I

GOING BACK

"What Is a Grown-Up Like Me Doing in a School Full of Kids?"

Do you belong in college?

Only you can answer the question, but if you are in doubt concerning your response, this chapter can help you discover the answer that is the right one for you.

The odds are that as an adult with responsibilities you have mixed feelings about adopting the student role. In the language of psychology, you are *ambivalent*. You want to go to school; you don't want to go to school. Like a latter-day Hamlet, you ask yourself, "To be a student or not to be a student? That is the question."

If you are in fact ambivalent about pursuing a college career, it is important to make up your mind. If you don't go to school, you may regret it for the rest of your life. If you do go to school, and it is not for you, you may be wasting your time and your money. A book by existential philosopher Søren Kierkegaard, *Either/Or*, makes the point that when we can't make a clear-cut choice between two alternatives we are mired in a kind of psychological mud. Like a car without four-wheel drive, we are stuck.

1

Clear thinking can act like a powerful transmission, however. Slowly we can find a direction, moving forward in life with determination and conviction.

In order to help you make a decision about whether or not you belong in college, let's examine some common misconceptions about higher education.

ELEVEN COMMON MISCONCEPTIONS

Misconception 1: College Is Only for Unusually Bright People

Becoming a college student requires normal intelligence, which, by definition, most people have. However, college students do not need to be "gifted," genetically superior, or endowed with unusual mental abilities. Most successful students, and most college graduates, are perfectly ordinary people in terms of memory, attention span, arithmetical understanding, comprehension of concepts, and other primary mental abilities. In fact, extraordinary intelligence sometimes *interferes* with academic performance because the student with such intelligence is easily bored or expects to obtain high grades without much effort.

Misconception 2: College Is Only for Unusually Creative People

This is an even greater falsehood than misconception 1. Intelligence is a measure of rational thinking. The core of rational thinking is its *convergent quality*, the ability to reach a single best answer given a set of premises. Creativity, on the other hand, is a measure of original thinking, thinking that has some element of novelty. The core of creativity is *divergent thinking*, thinking that will produce a different answer from the one given by others when there is a challenge to the mind or a problem to be solved. Based on taking many classes myself, and after numerous years of college teaching, I assure you that the last thing required of you in the great majority of classes is creativity. Relax. You need to *learn* in college, not invent ideas.

Misconception 3: You Have to Be Young to Go to College

Let's say you're inclined to ask yourself the question, "What's a grown-up like me doing in a school full of kids?" How should the question be answered?

Movies and television tend to portray most college students as recent escapees from adolescence. The adult in college is seen as an eccentric, a fish out of water, a kind of psychological outsider. Nothing can be further from the truth. If you are 25 years or older you will have plenty of companionship in many colleges. Small liberal arts colleges, where the majority of students live in dormitories and arrive shortly after graduating from high school, are the exception. However, at the great land grant colleges, the state universities, and the community colleges, the adult with responsibilities is the rule, not the exception. At the college where I teach, a two-year community college, the average age of a day student is 27. The average age of a part-time evening student is 29. And this is typical of many colleges.

The answer to the opening question, therefore, is, "The school is full of other grown-ups, or adults. You're not alone. You shouldn't feel like an outsider. What you're doing here is realistically working toward your academic goals and vocational dreams."

I am not satisfied with the unexplained word *adult*, and I want to spend some time defining it. I will return to this subject in the next section of this chapter.

Misconception 4: You Have to Have a Lot of Free Time to Go to College

This misconception is based on the familiar image of the full-time college student, the student who either lives at home or is enrolled in a residential college and is supported by parents. Again, this is an out-of-date, traditional image. A full-time college load, based on the semester system, is 15 units. This means that you only *sit in class* 15 hours a week even when you are taking a complete program. Of course, you are supposed to be studying two hours for every hour in class. So 15 units suggests a total investment of 45 hours a week.

Mary B. is a full-time homemaker with three children. Gary K. is a husband and father who is the sole supporter of his family; he works 40 hours a week in a grocery store. Pamela S. is a single parent raising two children; she works 20 hours a week as a waitress. Can any of these people go to college? It would seem that they don't have the time. *All of them are successful college students.* Their programs vary. Some go to classes only evenings. Others, like Pamela, are able to attend two mornings a week and one evening. None of them carry 15 units. It is best, when attending college part time, to take only two or three classes (6 to 9 units on the semester plan). If the class schedule can be arranged in terms of your work or family responsibilities, you can generally find times and places to study because this is done strictly on your own.

Misconception 5: It Takes a Lot of Money to Go to College

It is true, of course, that it takes some money to go to college. There are some basic costs, such as enrollment fees, tuition, and textbooks to buy. However, the average community college is subsidized by state and local taxes. Consequently, fees are low. The whole idea is to provide accessibility to people of average means. If money is very tight, and it often is, you can consult the college's financial aid office. There are both grants and loans available to most students. I am not talking about scholarships for exceptional individuals. I am talking about money that is available to the great majority of applicants. The school and the government *want* you to go to college. (There is more about financial aid in Chapter 4.)

And don't worry about clothes. The average college student wears casual everyday clothes. You don't have to have a "wardrobe" to go to college.

Misconception 6: It Takes a Long, Long Time to Complete a College Program

If you can afford to go to college full time, with summers off, you can earn either the standard Bachelor of Arts degree or Bachelor of Science degree in four years. By going during the summers and by taking more units, some students accomplish this in three years.

If you are going part time, as is almost certainly the way you will have to do it, add about 50 to 60 percent to the standard time. In other words, by going part time you will probably earn a bachelor's degree in six or seven years. This may sound a little discouraging at first. Pamela S., referred to earlier, is 26 years old. She told her counselor, "At the rate I'm going I'll be 32 years old when I graduate." She indicated that she was thinking of dropping out and letting go of some of her dreams. The counselor, a 40-year-old woman who had herself started college at the age of 27 and who now holds a Master of Arts degree in psychology, gently said, "Yes, you'll be 32 when you earn your college degree if you stay in school. And if you drop out, the time will pass anyway and you'll eventually be a 32-year-old woman without a college degree."

Not all college programs require the equivalent of four full-time years. Many community colleges offer Associate of Arts degrees that can be earned in the equivalent of two full-time years. These degrees open many job opportunities, depending on the subject matter major or area of concentration. Also, many community colleges offer certificate programs that require a limited number of courses. These certificate programs are generally in trade and vocational areas ranging from accounting to food-service management, from word processing to real estate appraising. Most of these certificate programs can be completed in less than the equivalent of two full-time years.

Misconception 7: You Have to Pass Entrance Examinations in Order to Go to College

Just before the U.S. Civil War began, young Horatio Alger, Jr., eventual author of many rags-to-riches novels, took entrance examinations for Harvard University. Two eight-hour days were devoted to the examinations, and he had to achieve satisfactory scores in such subject areas as algebra, geometry, Latin, and English.

Times have changed. Although high scores on standardized examinations such as the Scholastic Assessment Test (SAT) are required for direct admission to some state universities and selective private colleges, this is not true of community colleges.

It *is* true that in many cases you will have to *take* entrance examinations in order to enroll in courses at a community college. But, believe it or not, you don't have to pass them with scores defined in advance. At many, perhaps most, community colleges, your examination scores are strictly for advisory purposes. You don't have to abide by them. It is becoming increasingly difficult for counselors and colleges to enforce mandatory assignment to classes based on verbal and mathematical scores obtained on standardized tests. Some people claim that the scores discriminate unfairly against members of racial and ethnic minorities as well as nontraditional students. Also, the standardized tests are neither absolutely valid nor completely reliable.

If you do want to use the information from a standardized test as advisory in nature, many colleges offer remedial courses in English, arithmetic, and other basic skills that make it possible to increase these skills and thus take courses that will count toward a degree program. You will find that the vast majority of community colleges have what is known as an *open door* policy, meaning that all applicants are welcome.

If you do your first two years of college work toward a bachelor's degree at a community college, which I recommend for most adult students, you will find that your work will transfer to a university or four-year college. The four-year institutions have agreements with the two-year ones, and you can enter with third-year (i.e., junior) standing without entrance examinations. I know this sounds too good to be true, but look into it. You'll find that what I'm telling you is so.

Misconception 8: You Need to Know What You Want in Order to Go to College

You *do* have to declare a major, don't you? You have to say that you are majoring in psychology, history, chemistry, biology, or something else, don't you? Well, this is not as important as the beginning student thinks. In the first place, if you don't know what area you really want to pursue, you can often declare something general such as Liberal Arts. This is perfectly acceptable, and you can then take almost anything you want to take. In the second place, if you are aiming toward an eventual bachelor's degree, the first two years of college are taken up primarily by general education requirements. These are courses in the social sciences, the life sciences, the physical sciences, English composition, mathematics, and sometimes a foreign language. In most cases you will not have to take more than two or three courses in your major in your first two years of college. And you can change your major readily after you complete your first two years of work.

The truth is that many students use the first two years of college as a way of *discovering* what they want to major in. The large array of general education courses may be looked on something like a smörgasbord. You *sample* courses, and find out what is to your taste. You consequently receive the information that makes it possible for you to follow a line of study leading to a vocation or profession that is compatible with your talents, interests, and personality.

Misconception 9: Professors Tend to Be Hostile to the Older, Nontraditional Student

This misconception has been perpetuated by several movies that have portrayed college professors as aloof, cold, and distant. In addition, the authoritarian professor makes a laughing stock, a kind of psychological scapegoat, out of the underprepared adult student. The attitude conveyed seems to be, "You really don't belong here. You're wasting my time."

This portrayal is *completely distorted*. The great majority of college professors look upon their work as not merely a job, but as a high calling. Teachers live to teach. They want to help you succeed. They really do. If you, the student, demonstrate a genuine will to learn, the professor will usually find this both exciting and rewarding. Rent a videotape of the movie *Educating Rita* with Michael Caine and Julie Walters. Rita is a married woman with an enormous vitality and a will to learn. The professor teaches English literature and is able to provide her with understanding as well as the kind of ideas and information she needs. I am not exaggerating when I say that there are many more professors like Michael Caine's character in the movie than cold, hostile ones. In brief, the professor is on your side. He or she wants to see you succeed.

Misconception 10: College Graduates Don't Really Earn That Much More Money Than Noncollege Graduates

It is true that many individuals who are not college graduates make more money than many individuals who are. We all know of cases in which a person goes into a business such as a restaurant, a mail-order enterprise, a plumbing company, a dry-cleaning store, or general contracting, and earns two or three times as much money as the average individual. I am quick to agree that a high level of education is not the only road to financial success in the United States.

It is also true, however, that the average college graduate earns about twice as much money per year than the average high school graduate. Taking 1990 as a baseline, a U.S. Census Bureau study reported that the average high school graduate earned a little over $12,000 per year. The average college graduate earned a little over $24,000 per year, a difference of $12,000. Even if you start your career late, say around age 35, you still have 30 working years ahead of you. Thirty multiplied by $12,000 equals $360,000. That's quite a bit of money. (Allowing for inflation over a 30-year period, the actual dollars could be $500,000 or more.)

Misconception 11: You Will Be Neglecting Your Children If You Go to College

If you are the kind of person who will neglect your children, you will probably neglect them whether you go to college or not. If you are a responsible parent, you will go to college and arrange for day care or other caregiving when you have to attend classes. When you are with your children you will give them the time, love, and attention they need. I have known hundreds of parents who have gone to college, and on the whole they are *better* parents as a result of their college experience. They have more to give their children because their own mental and emotional needs are nurtured. And they provide inspiring role models for their children. To a large extent children learn by a process called *observational learning*, in which they tend to copy the behavior of someone they admire. You won't be slighting them by seeking higher education. It is more likely that you will be opening a pathway.

WHO IS AN ADULT?

Until now I have been using the word *adult* as an undefined term. I assume that you are one, and that if you are you know it. Nonetheless, there is some merit in exploring the meaning of the concept briefly.

Note that I used the word *concept* in the prior sentence. Adulthood is just that, a *concept.* For example, in primitive tribes one had adult status upon reaching puberty. At 13 or 14 years of age males became warriors and hunters; females became wives and mothers. Incidentally, this was not done from ignorance or stupidity. Anthropologists point out that it was absolutely necessary for survival.

The Industrial Revolution brought about the concept of *adolescence*, a protracted period after puberty. In our culture this has generally spanned the years from about 13 to 18. And it is generally agreed that one is a biological adult at age 18. However, is one a mental and emotional adult?

Some people are; others aren't. If you are responsible and independent, then you are an adult. If you are irresponsible and dependent, you are still an emotional adolescent.

Narrowly defined, all students in college are biological adults because they are usually at least 18 years of age. In your case, however, I imagine additional possibilities. These include: (1) being married or in a committed relationship, (2) being a parent in a traditional household, (3) being a single parent, (4) working 20 to 40 hours a week at a job, or (5) perceiving yourself as significantly older than the other students. Some of these, of course, overlap.

Age in and of itself is not the only defining attribute of who is and who is not an adult. For example, Sebastian D., age 24, lives at home with his parents. His father is a prosperous physician who encourages higher education. Sebastian drives an expensive sports car, has a generous allowance, earns mostly Cs and Ds, and drops out of many classes. He can't seem to get himself motivated, even though he is bright. Sebastian is not an adult in the mental and emotional sense.

On the other hand, Leona B. married when she was 17 years of age, had two children in two years, maintains a household, and takes two college classes. She is busy, but she is organized. She enjoys her family and her college career. Although she is only 20, Leona is a mental and emotional adult. She feels older than other students who have the same chronological age. And it is easy to see why.

In short, the use of the word *adult* in this book implies that you have reached a certain level of mental and emotional maturity, regardless of your chronological age. In primitive tribes, to become an adult was a *status*, a formal position in the tribe. The psychology has not changed. An adult is still a person with a kind of status within our culture. If the individual is responsible and has responsibilities, then he or she is an adult. Others look in your direction and see someone who can carry his or her share of the load.

Do adults belong in college? Yes, of course. Not only do they belong in college, they also tend to be the *best* college students because they want to be there and they are motivated. On the whole, adults in college are a joy to teach. And the vast majority of professors will agree with this statement.

So don't let the fact that you see yourself as an adult—or are over 25—hold you back in the slightest. It's not an impediment. It's an asset.

A TALE OF TWO STUDENTS

I am going to tell you a short story about two students. I will reveal my reasons for telling this tale to you at its end.

Student 1 liked to read—but he read mostly comic books, action/adventure novels, and science fiction magazines. He received a D in ninth-grade algebra and failing notices in tenth-grade Latin. As a senior in high school he avoided the college-preparation physics course because he had no confidence in his ability to do the required mathematics. (He had developed the attitude of *learned helplessness* toward the subject area of mathematics. There is more about learned helplessness in Chapter 13.) In his third year of college he scored in the 6th percentile *toward the bottom* in a pre-test designed to evaluate readiness to take a statistics course required of behavioral science majors. Student 1 was often bored in high school and college. He had no well-defined academic or vocational goals, but he daydreamed about writing science fiction novels someday. Although he graduated from college, he had a mediocre C+ average and felt completely unqualified for any professional school or graduate training.

Student 2 earned an A or a B in almost every graduate course he took. He enrolled in several courses in advanced statistics, and he substituted a special examination in statistics in place of one foreign language examination in partial satisfaction of the requirements for a Ph.D. degree. He was 28 years of age when he embarked on his graduate training, and it took 10 years to complete his program because he had family responsibilities. Student 2 was usually interested in his classes. He is now the author of a number of psychology books distributed by major publishers.

The name of Student 1 is Frank J. Bruno—my name. And—you guessed it—the name of Student 2 is also my own. However, it *is* correct to say that Student 1 and Student 2 were two *different* students, even though both of them have the same name. Student 1 was Frank J. Bruno from the ages of 14 to 21. Student 2 was Frank J. Bruno from the ages of 28 to 38. The adolescent and the adult were dissimilar in important ways. They had neither the same motives nor the same attitudes.

Why have I related my own story? What point or points do I want to make? First, if I, with my early motivational problems and academic deficiencies, was able to succeed eventually as a student, this provides rather basic evidence that you too may someday be able to tell a similar story. Second, I know what it is to go to school as an adult with responsibilities. Third, I have something to relate to you derived from my own academic struggles. What I have learned will be of real value to you. In this book I talk to you as one who has muddled and struggled through to some modest measure of success. The book is based on solid learning theory in psychology, but it is also a practical book grounded in my own experience.

CONCLUDING REMARKS

Do you belong in college? As I said at the beginning of the chapter, I can't answer for you; only you can answer for yourself. However, I have tried to show you that many of the reasons that you might bring forth for answering "no" are based on misconceptions. These misconceptions act as barriers to realizing your full potential as a student and human being. But these misconceptions are only *psychological barriers*. They have no more substance than ghosts. Also, I have tried to encourage you with my own example in "A Tale of Two Students." If there was anyone who was underprepared for college work it was me. And yet I was eventually able to become an effective student.

I admit that I have tried to load the dice in favor of a *yes* answer. Very few people regret going to college. I almost never meet a person who says, "Darn it. I'm a college graduate. I sure wish I didn't have a B.A." I often meet people who say, "I should have gone to college. I could have made more out my life."

I hope you decide to say *yes* to your dreams and your talents.

I hope you decide to say *yes* to yourself.

KEY POINTS TO REMEMBER

- The odds are that as an adult with responsibilities you have mixed feelings about adopting the student role.
- In order to help you make a decision about whether or not you belong in college it is helpful to examine some common misconceptions about higher education.
- The chapter presented 11 common misconceptions, such as *College is only for unusually bright people* and *College is only for unusually creative people.* It was demonstrated that these, and other, misconceptions are based on false assumptions.

- The use of the word *adult* in this book implies that you have reached a certain level of mental and emotional maturity, regardless of your chronological age.
- "A Tale of Two Students" is a true story based on my own experience. It provides basic evidence that early motivational problems and academic deficiencies can be overcome.
- Misconceptions about higher education are psychological barriers to academic success. They have no more substance than ghosts.
- You are encouraged to say *yes* to your dreams and your talents.

2

BEFORE YOU GO BACK

What You Need to Know

When Dorothy is carried by a cyclone into the incredible land of Oz she suffers a long period of confusion. At first she makes decisions that make matters worse. Gradually she becomes oriented and effective through the help and wise counsel of the Scarecrow, the Tin Man, the Cowardly Lion, the Good Witch Glinda, and eventually the Great Wizard, Oz himself.

As you stand outside of the walls of the academic world, it may seem to you that college, like Oz, is a strange, forbidden land. It is *not* forbidden. You have a right to go to college. You *belong* there if you *want* to be there. I hope that this point was settled to your satisfaction in Chapter 1.

The world of college is in some ways a new and confusing one, however. And you, like Dorothy, need orientation. To some extent this will be forthcoming as a part of the educational process. Friendly guides in the form of counselors, teachers, admissions officers, and so forth *will* appear. Yes, a few of these people will be inept and may confuse you, but on the whole they will be helpful. And you will gradually learn your way around.

It is desirable to become pre-oriented *toward* college before you become oriented *in* college. You don't want to find yourself landing, as if thrust by a psychological cyclone, into a situation that is ill-defined and filled with unexpected pitfalls. That is what this chapter is for. As the title indicates, before you go back, there are some things worth knowing.

KINDS OF COLLEGES

It is important that you have some information about the kinds of colleges that exist in order to select the one that is right in terms of your personal needs.

Universities

As institutions, universities stand at the top of the academic ladder. Universities can also be called "colleges," but the very word *university* suggests a large school with a great diversity of offerings. Maybe a brief, and relatively accurate, definition of a university is simply this: a large college. Universities are often state supported. An example is the University of California with its several branch campuses.

Some universities define themselves as containing several colleges, such as the College of Law, the College of Liberal Arts, or the College of Sciences. Consequently, an alternative definition of a university is: a cluster, or collection, of colleges.

Universities offer a four-year degree. This is either a Bachelor of Arts or a Bachelor of Science, and it is usually the degree implied when it is said that someone is a "college graduate." Universities also offer a Master's degree. This requires one or two years of academic credit past the Bachelor's. Some universities, about half of them, offer a Doctorate (Ph.D.) in various fields of study. This requires a few more years of academic credit past the Master's.

If you are going back to college with no prior college work, in most cases you should be considering applying directly to a university only if you have an excellent high school record. An attractive alternative is to transfer to a university after you have completed two years of work at a different kind of college, such as a community college. Generally, your two years of work will be accepted for full credit toward the Bachelor's degree, and you will lose no time overall.

Colleges

If the unadorned word *college* is used without an adjective in front of it, such as "community" or "vocational," then the implication is that the institution in question is a four-year one and has the right to grant a Bachelor's degree. The right to earn higher degrees may or may not be offered. Colleges tend to be smaller than universities and frequently have a more restricted range of offerings. Consequently, colleges are often somewhat specialized. *Liberal arts colleges* are likely to offer degrees with concentrations of study in such fields as psychology, history, politics, philosophy, literature, foreign languages, fine arts, and so forth. *Scientific* or *technical* colleges are likely to offer degrees with concentrations of study in such fields as mathematics, physics, engineering, astronomy, architecture, and so forth. It should be noted that in practice, however, the distinction between liberal arts and scientific colleges often blurs, and the two types often overlap with similar offerings.

Many colleges are state supported. At the same time, however, many are private institutions supported by a combination of endowments, alumni contributions, investments, and tuition charges.

Vocational Colleges

Vocational colleges exist to train students in a highly specific career field such as commercial illustration, accounting, advertising, law, real estate, insurance, cosmetology, journalism, film making, acting, and so forth. Most of these institutions are private and charge tuition. The entire course of study is often two years or less in length. Many vocational colleges are fine institutions with formal accreditation, but many others are simply self-proclaimed colleges. These have been nicknamed "storefront schools." The degrees they offer are not recognized by other colleges. Consequently the value and status of such degrees is often questionable. The careful student should be on guard and thoroughly explore the reputation of a vocational college before attending it.

Community Colleges

Community colleges are usually fully accredited two-year institutions supported by a combination of state funds and local taxes. Sometimes they are referred to as *junior colleges*. The adjective "junior" was once used to indicate that such colleges offered only lower-division work (i.e., the first two years of college) and prepared the student to transfer credits to a four-year college where a Bachelor's degree could be completed. The word "junior" has acquired the unfortunate connotation of an inferior status, and consequently the preferred contemporary usage is "community." The implication is that the two-year institution serves the needs of a local community.

Community colleges offer a two-year program leading to either an Associate of Arts or an Associate of Science degree. The student who earns such a degree can go on to complete a Bachelor's degree in two more years of work at a four-year institution.

In addition to the Associate's degree, community colleges offer many vocational certificate programs that can be completed in two years or less. Thus one can earn a certificate in such fields as administration of justice, real estate, word processing, air conditioning, automotive, early childhood development, drug and rehabilitation counseling, psychiatric assistance, and escrow. These certificate programs are practical, relatively short courses of study that lead directly to jobs.

Although community colleges charge tuition, the cost of tuition is generally quite a bit lower than that associated with four-year colleges and universities.

In most cases, if you are returning to college after 25 and have responsibilities, a community college is your best bet. It is close to home. You can come and go as you wish, make your own hours, and even attend part time. The credits you earn are fully transferable to a four-year college. The community college is a good first stepping-stone for the returning student.

WHOM TO CONTACT

Let's assume that you are standing on the campus of a college that you have decided to attend. Where do you go? You are alone and need guidance. Ask the first passerby for directions to the Administration Building. Don't feel shy or intimidated, because it's not a stupid question. Newcomers who need orientation are common on any campus. They arrive almost every day. A friendly student or teacher will direct you.

In the hall of the Administration Building you will see signs over doorways with labels such as "President's Office," "Dean of Instruction," "Evening Division," "Records," "Admissions," "Financial Aid," and "Counseling." Although you might think it's the Admissions Office you want, head for the Counseling Office.

The first person you meet will be a student assistant, full-time clerk, or the Counseling Office secretary. Indicate that you are thinking of going back to school, that you have been out of the academic flow for a while, and that you need to see a counselor for some guidance. Let's assume that you are given an appointment one hour in the future. At this point you can get a good feeling for the campus and the kind of students that attend the college by going to the snack bar in the Student Center. (Again, ask directions. I won't keep repeating this but will assume from here on that you will ask for directions when you need to.)

Before we go on, note that you will be given an appointment to see a counselor. Usually what I have described will be the case, but you may in fact be given an appointment for a few days in the future. Therefore, now that you know you need to contact the Counseling Office first, an option is to telephone ahead for an appointment before you actually go to the campus.

The counselor you meet will talk to you, one to one, in a private office for a half-hour to a full hour. He or she will typically have a Master's degree in counseling psychology, educational psychology, or a similar field. In the vast majority of cases, counselors will be helpful and well informed. Guiding students is what they do all day, every day.

WHAT WILL BE EXPECTED OF YOU

Your counselor, whom you will probably see more than once, will tell you what will be expected of you in order to gain admission as a student. If you are planning to attend a community college, you will be accepted as a student if you are over 18, even if you don't have a high school diploma. However, testing in verbal and quantitative skills with an instrument such as the Scholastic Assessment Test (SAT) will be scheduled. And this information will be useful in deciding what courses you need to take first.

If you are planning to attend a university or a four-year college, you will usually have to present an above-average high school academic record in order to gain direct admission.

In either event, one thing that will be required is that you obtain a copy of your high school transcript and present it when you apply for formal admission. If you are attending a tax-funded public institution, you will need to provide proof that you are a resident of the state. If you are not, substantial nonresident fees are charged.

Your counselor will also provide you with a current college catalog. Hang on to this book and get to know it. It is, in essence, the school's contract with you. It tells you what the school expects of you in the way of graduation requirements, credits, attendance, and so forth. It also sets forth brief descriptions of all of the classes offered. If you enroll, you will be expected to be familiar with the catalog and its provisions.

In addition to the catalog, your counselor will provide you with a copy of the schedule of classes for the coming semester or quarter. The schedule sets forth a detailed listing of when and where all the classes meet, including both day and evening classes. The last names of instructors who teach the classes are also indicated. Later, when you get to know other students, you will find out that there is a grapevine that provides informal information on the traits of various teachers.

Before you leave the counselor's office, be sure to obtain the counselor's telephone number and hours available for appointment.

ALTERNATIVE ADMISSIONS PROGRAMS

Let's say that your high school record is undistinguished. Now that you are 25 years of age or older you look back and realize that you were an undermotivated adolescent, but a number of years have passed and now you are a different person. However, you are not qualified to enter a four-year college or university. Are there alternative admissions programs for students like you? There certainly are. More than one institution will offer you a chance to make a new start.

An *alternative admissions program* consists of a policy that allows applicants who do not come up to usual academic criteria to gain admission. Of course, the largest single alternative admissions program is the one provided by the community college system. As I have already indicated, if you complete two years of lower-division college work at a community college, you can gain full upper-division status at a four-year institution.

More and more four-year institutions are *directly* opening the door to beginning students they would not have admitted in the past, however. The idea is to *encourage* the adult who wants to go to college, not to slam a door in his or her face. Here are some conditions under which you might qualify for a particular school's alternative admissions program:

1. Your high school grades were only average, but you have high scores on the Scholastic Assessment Test (SAT). This shows that you have the capacity for college work.
2. You have been out of school for a few years and you have a history of stable employment. This demonstrates that you have the capacity to stick to a task, a trait that is very important in college students.
3. You are a parent. You have a major responsibility in life, and it is likely you will be motivated to achieve a goal that will improve the quality of both your life and your child's. A number of institutions provide day-care facilities for preschoolers.
4. You are a member of a racial or ethnic minority. Some colleges and universities encourage affirmative action as a component in their overall alternative admissions program.

5. You took challenging courses in high school such as physics, calculus, or a foreign language. Possibly your overall grade point average is not high because you grappled with difficult subjects. Also, you have demonstrated the capacity to take on courses with some real academic content.

6. You make a good impression on a counselor in an interview. You set forth your case well, and you convince the counselor that you have the potential to make an effective student. It helps to have a well-defined field of study in mind. The student who says, "I don't know what I want to major in. I just want to explore courses for a while," is not as well regarded as the student who says, "I want to work toward a career in child development. I have always dreamed of working with children." A recommendation from the counselor may make the difference and tip the scale in your favor. (If you do not in fact have a well-defined field of study in mind, this is understandable. If you want to explore alternatives, and evaluate options, it is probably better to do it at a community college than at a four-year institution.)

7. You are able to provide at least two letters of recommendation from persons whose opinions mean something. For example, one letter can come from a former high school teacher who was impressed with your abilities. A second letter can come from a person who already works in an occupation associated with your projected field of study.

8. You have an impressive record of extracurricular activity in high school, such as participation in dramatic performances, glee club, band, student government, the school paper, or sports.

Of course, different institutions have different criteria. You can get the information you need by phoning or visiting the Admissions Office of a four-year college and inquiring about their alternative admissions program.

TUITION, FEES, AND OTHER COSTS

It takes money to go to college. Information concerning financial aid is provided in Chapter 4. For the present, let's concern ourselves with the costs themselves.

The first and most important cost is *tuition*, the basic charge made for formal instruction by a college. Please note that fees vary widely from state to state, and the figures presented here are averages. Tuition at a community college is approximately $400 to $500 per year for a full-time student.

Tuition at a state four-year college is approximately $1,200 to $1,600 per year. Tuition at a state university is approximately $2,500 to $3,500 per year.

At this point tuition takes a big leap upwards. Tuition at a private four-year college is approximately $12,000 to $14,000 per year.

Of course, if you are attending on a part-time basis, your annual tuition will be considerably less. You will be charged on a reduced pro-rata basis depending on the number of units you register for. For example, a student taking two classes, or six units on the semester system, will pay at a community college about $100 for a given semester.

In addition to tuition, there are fees. Fees may include those for student services, accident insurance, health services, parking, and grade mailing. Miscellaneous fees such as these may total approximately $100 to $200 per year.

Textbooks are required in most courses. The cost of textbooks for a single course can vary from about $35 to $50. If you are taking a full academic load (five courses), your textbooks for one semester will cost you about $175 to $250.

Students who reside at a college and live in a dormitory can expect to pay an additional $4,000 to $6,000 per year for room and board.

If you are an out-of-state student and decide to attend a state-supported institution, there is often a nonresident tuition. This can be as high as $2,000 to $4,000 per year for a full-time student.

PART-TIME AND FULL-TIME PROGRAMS

The vast majority of state-funded colleges and universities do not require full-time attendance. Many small private colleges, catering primarily to high-achieving students recently graduated from high school, do require full-time attendance.

The fact that you can go to college on a part-time basis is a tremendous advantage. This means that if you only take two or three classes a semester, you can take them in a block—for example, all in the morning, all in the afternoon, or even all in the evening. For the adult with responsibilities, you can continue to work part time and also meet the demands of your partner or children. A realistic plan that has worked for many motivated students is to enroll for three courses instead of the usual five. Often you will find it is possible to do this and to work at a job for about 25 hours per week. You can also take one or two summer-session courses every summer. By following this plan, you can earn a Bachelor's degree in about five or six years instead of the usual four. So it need not take "forever" to reach a goal even if you are a part-time student.

QUESTIONS TO ASK

Don't be afraid to ask questions! No question is stupid. Nor should you be ashamed because you have to ask questions. And *keep asking* until the answer is clear to you. Often the first answer is inadequate and based on assumptions with which you are not familiar. You will be asking questions of counselors, teachers, secretaries, and clerks in various offices. On the whole, these people will be helpful. The questions that you need to ask are the ones that are relevant to your needs, and you will have many questions I can't anticipate. However, below are examples of some of the kinds of questions you will want to ask.

1. Do I have to take a Scholastic Assessment Test (SAT) before I can enroll? Do I have to abide by recommendations based on the test?
2. How much is tuition?
3. Can I attend on a part-time basis?
4. Do you have a day-care center?
5. Can I drop classes without academic penalty if I am unhappy with my performance? Or do I have to stay enrolled in the class even if I am doing D or F work?
6. What is the school's attendance policy?
7. Is your institution fully accredited?

CONCLUDING REMARKS

It can be threatening even to *think* about going back to school after you have been out of the system for a while. Just imagining yourself on a college campus and talking to a counselor may raise your blood pressure a few points and bring sweat to your palms. If it's any comfort, you are not alone in this reaction. Venturing forth in the direction of undiscovered territory is always fear arousing, but it can also have an element of positive excitement and challenge. Just keep in mind that as you gather information your anxiety will be reduced. The more your questions are answered, the more you will know what you are doing and why you are doing it.

I have tried to preorient you a bit here. I hope that this will give you confidence to take the actual step of applying for admission to the college of your choice. This is the subject matter of Chapter 3.

KEY POINTS TO REMEMBER

- Universities are large institutions that offer the Bachelor's degree, the Master's degree, and, usually, the Doctorate (Ph.D.).
- The unadorned word *college* without an adjective in front of it such as "community" or "vocational" implies that the institution in question is a four-year one. Colleges tend to be smaller than universities.
- Vocational colleges exist to train students in highly specific career fields.
- Community colleges are usually fully accredited two-year institutions. The first two years of academic work can be completed at such a college in preparation for transfer to a four-year college.
- If you are a newcomer on a college campus, do not hesitate to ask for directions. The first place you want to go to is the Administration Building.
- The first office you want to go to is the Counseling Office. And the first important person to contact is a counselor.
- If you are planning to attend a community college, you will be accepted as a student if you are over 18 even if you don't have a high school diploma.
- Become familiar with the college catalog and the schedule of classes for the coming semester or quarter.
- An *alternative admissions program* consists of a policy that allows applicants who do not come up to the usual academic criteria to gain admission directly to a four-year institution.
- *Tuition* is the basic charge made for formal instruction by a college. In addition to regular tuition, other costs may include nonresident tuition, fees, and the price of textbooks. A charge for room and board is made to dormitory residents.
- The vast majority of state-funded colleges and universities do not require full-time attendance.
- Don't hesitate to ask questions. It is a natural part of the orientation process.

3

GETTING IN

*Key Steps in the
Admissions Procedure*

You have made the big decision. You *are* going back. You *will* be a college student.

You have explored the options open to you and you have studied several college catalogs. And you have made a choice. You have decided on which college to go to.

What do you do now?

CONTACTING A COLLEGE

Call or visit the Counseling Office. I assume that you have made one prior visit to the school and have talked to a counselor, as was discussed in Chapter 2. I advised you to remember that person's name. If you have, and if you seemed to get along well, ask for a second appointment with that counselor. If the relationship did not seem to click, then, of course, ask for somebody else. (Don't hesitate to do this.)

If this is your first contact with the college, do as I suggested in Chapter 2. Make an appointment to see a counselor because an effective counselor will be your primary source of orientation information. Obtain basic information in the first half of the interview (see Chapter 2).

Let's assume that you are past the preliminaries. Now you are ready to settle down and talk about actual admission to the school.

The first and most important decisions you must make can be summarized in the form of two questions: (1) How many classes should you take? (2) What classes should you take?

Let's address each question individually. If you are going to college for the first time, it is a good idea to avoid biting off more than you can chew. I have seen more than one returning student sign up for a full academic load (five courses or 15 semester units) while trying to raise children and work part time. Frequently these students end up dropping several classes, or worse yet, earning poor grades. Don't let this happen to you.

(At this point let's make a distinction between the semester system and the quarter system. The *semester system* is the one used by the vast majority of colleges. There are two semesters in the academic year. A full load is 15 units, and the typical course is 3 units. It requires the equivalent of a total of 8 academic semesters to graduate with a four-year degree. In terms of units, the sum is 120. The *quarter system* is divided into four quarters per calendar year. The equivalent of an academic year in the quarter system is *three* quarters. Consequently, it takes both more courses completed as well as quarter-units in order to graduate on the quarter system. However, the total amount of both academic work and time spent in school are about the same with either system. In order to avoid confusion, my examples in this book are all based on the semester system.)

My own advice is to sign up for no more than two or three courses the first semester you return to school. You can always increase the study load if you have the capacity to do so.

At some point your counselor will probably ask you a crucial question: "What do you want to major in?"

Both your task and the counselor's are made much easier if you have a definite idea of what you want to major in, such as psychology, accounting, or architecture. A *major* is a principal focus of study. Some colleges call it a *concentration*. In the case of most popular majors, the counselor will have a list ready that gives the courses recommended to complete the major. Some of these courses will be in the major itself. Other courses will be general education courses that count toward graduation or transfer and that have been selected to be somewhat related to your major. For example, if you are majoring in psychology, a required science course might be biology. And if you are majoring in architecture, a required science course might be physics.

On the other hand, you may have only a vague idea of what you want to major in. You will need to take placement tests, complete courses required for graduation, and explore electives in order to make a final determination. Consequently, you may find yourself spinning your wheels and taking unnecessary courses. However, it is better to do this than to go too far down the wrong road.

In any event, you have decided to go back to school. You have made your first contact with the college through the counselor. Working together, the two of you have drawn up a tentative schedule of classes. And now you are ready to apply for formal admission.

HOW TO APPLY FOR ADMISSION

You will need to go to the Admissions Office, and you will almost certainly be directed there by the counselor. (In some cases you will have to apply for admission first before a counselor will take the time to help you draw up a schedule of classes. The sequence of events in an actual case, therefore, might be somewhat different from that described here.) When you arrive at the Admissions Office you will encounter a clerk who will give you the admissions forms. If you like, you can take these forms home and fill them out at your leisure, without pressure.

The admissions forms are usually relatively easy to fill out, and they require only information that you generally have at your fingertips—such as your name, social security number, date of birth, home address, and so forth.

When you return the forms and file them with the Admissions Office, you will be required to provide identification in the form of a driver's license or social security card and to order a high school transcript be sent to the college. As earlier indicated, if you are a nonresident of the state, there will be a special fee.

Once your admissions forms are filed and accepted, and your fees are paid, you can consider yourself to be admitted to the college. You are a member of the student body.

Now your two principal tasks are to register for classes and to take placement tests. In most schools these days, if you have applied for admission early enough you will be given a registration date. This will make it possible for you to avoid a long wait in line for classes. Even under these conditions, be prepared for some lines and some waiting. Contemporary registration procedures have been streamlined, however, and with the aid of computers events usually proceed rapidly. If you have applied late, which is often the case if you are going back to school for the first time, you may not get an ideal appointment date and you will run into the problem of closed classes.

If some of the classes in your proposed schedule are closed, don't despair. There are usually counselors and faculty members on standby who have lists of open and closed classes. These individuals will help you adapt your schedule. Usually the problem of closed classes is worst the first time you register. In the future you can make it a point to register early, and you will get all or most of the classes you need.

Even if a class is closed, and you want it badly, all is not lost. In many colleges students often appear on the first day of class with the hope of being added. Adding you to the roll is usually at the discretion of the instructor. If there are seats available, and if the instructor is willing to add students, then he or she can sign an add form, and you will become a member of the class. This is a chancy procedure, however. The probability that you will be added cannot be stated in the individual case, as it depends on how many people want to be added, the educational philosophy of the instructor, and so forth. However, it doesn't hurt to try if it's important to you.

At some point in the admissions procedure you will be scheduled to take a placement test. The purpose of this test, or group of tests in some cases, is to assess your skills and aptitudes. It is probably a good idea to take the placement test or tests *before* you register for classes, or you may find yourself swimming in academic water that is over your head. Consequently, the sequence of events described earlier may have also included testing. However, in some colleges, because of the crush of new admissions, placement testing will take place during your first semester.

In the past the taking of tests was mandatory. For example, a particular college might have required that a student score in the 65th percentile or higher as a requirement for a social science class with credit toward a four-year degree. As earlier indicated, however, today both the reliability and validity of the tests have been called into question. Some observers have leveled the charge that the tests often discriminate unfairly against racial and ethnic minority students because of subtle, built-in biases in the tests. Consequently, the prevailing present attitude is to take the results of the tests on a advisory basis only. In discussions with a counselor, a student is usually free to make his or her own decisions concerning the choice of a major, what courses to take, a class schedule, and how many units to attempt. The test results are considered to be useful, but they are not the Hand of Fate. In a subsequent section of this chapter I give advice on the taking of placement tests.

GETTING ORIENTED

I remember when I was in the seventh grade at Washington Irving Junior High School in Glendale, California, the homeroom teacher kept talking about "orientation." I didn't have the slightest idea what she meant, and I didn't ask. I thought the word had something to do with sailing east, toward the mysterious Orient. I needed orientation toward the word *orient*!

In a sense the word *orient* does in fact have something to do with sailing east. The ancient mariners did not have good directions for the sea passage to countries east of Europe. They needed guidance and better maps. It turns out that the word orient is derived from a very old word meaning "rising sun." And the sun rises in the East. Consequently, the word *orient* gradually acquired meanings such as "getting good directions" or "knowing where you are and where you are going."

It *is* important to get oriented. Put another way, if you are not oriented, your behavior will resemble that of the proverbial chicken with its head chopped off.

One of the first things you want to do is to get acquainted with the college campus. Your catalog or schedule of classes will almost certainly contain a map of the campus. If not, obtain one from the Counseling Office. Walk around and get familiar with the locations of buildings and offices. Find out where, for example, the Infirmary or Health Center is. You may need its services in a medical emergency. Find out the location of Campus Security. Most colleges now have a small police force. You may need the services of an officer at some point in the future. If you have a car, you may visit this office early in your college career in order to obtain a parking sticker. (Yes, this often requires another fee.)

Take a walk to the Library. Familiarize yourself with its hours and regulations and obtain a library card. I hope you intend to spend some time there. It is usually a good place to study because it is quiet, and you will seldom be bothered. Effective students also tend to check out books and do collateral reading.

I referred to the Student Center earlier. This usually has a snack bar and a recreation area. It is a good place to meet other students, as it is a place where friends go to socialize. However, the charms of the Student Center can be seductive, and it is possible to waste a lot of time there. So enjoy the Student Center, but be aware of its risks.

A very important part of your orientation can be accomplished by studying the college catalog. I mentioned earlier that this is the school's contract with you. The institution *will* abide by the statements made in the catalog. If, for example, a counselor contradicts the catalog, and you are puzzled, it is almost certainly the counselor who is wrong. There's no need to be puzzled, really. The authority of the catalog supersedes the authority of the counselor.

Many students neglect this phase of orientation. It is a big mistake. The information in the catalog is essential. For example, it will set forth the college's mission, its accreditation status, the attendance policy, grading policy, a policy on credit by examination only, the conditions of academic probation and dismissal, a policy on repetition of course work, the procedure for filing a student grievance, and so forth. This is all information that you need to know or that you need to be able to obtain readily. In addition to the items already indicated, the catalog will contain a *complete* list of all courses offered by the college, including brief descriptions.

Some colleges require that all beginning students take a one-unit orientation course. Typically this course meets one hour a week for eight weeks. The information you obtain in an orientation course is pure gold. Studies have shown that students who take the orientation course are less likely to drop out of college than students who have not taken it. If your college doesn't require the course, it almost certainly offers it. I recommend taking it. It will pay off in both the near and far future.

TAKING PLACEMENT TESTS

Before you take a placement test you should know *why* you are taking the test. And in order to know this, you need to know what the test seeks to measure.

First, let's state what placement tests *are not*. Placement tests are not measurements of intelligence, creativity, or personality.

Placement tests fall into a general category of testing known as *educational testing*. The goal of placement tests is to measure your *skill level*, how well you can perform, in three critical areas: reading, English, and mathematics. Reading and English might sound as if they are the same, but ability in reading refers primarily to comprehension. It is important to be able to understand, for example, what textbooks say. On the other hand, ability in English refers primarily to the ability to *perform* certain skills such as spelling correctly, punctuating properly, and writing coherent sentences and paragraphs.

Probably the educational test best known to the general public is the Scholastic Assessment Test (SAT). In addition, there are other educational tests such as the test battery of the American College Testing Program (ACT) and the College Qualification Tests (CQT).

Test results are often reported in terms of *percentiles*. A percentile score utilizes a base of 100. For example, if you score in the 70th percentile on the Verbal Scale of the SAT, this means that based on a standardized population of subjects who have already taken the test, you are above 70 percent of them. Or, put differently, you are in the top 30 percent.

Let's return to the basic question of *why* you are taking the tests. You are being asked to take the tests in order to obtain information that will help you succeed in college. It's almost that simple.

I say it's *almost* that simple because this is true only *if* you have already been accepted for admission. If you are applying for admission to a highly selective college, however, then it is true that a placement test result is frequently used as a screening device. If your scores are too low, you will be deemed unlikely to succeed at that institution, and your application may be rejected. Because of this screening function, there have arisen preparatory courses. For a fee, you can learn "tricks of the trade" that will help you obtain better placement test scores. Also, there are many excellent books available that give test-taking hints and practice examinations. These are quite popular and easy to obtain in both libraries and bookstores.

However, if you have already been accepted for admission, which is often the case, the idea is not to play a game with those who seek to advise and guide you. Consequently, you are often told that you cannot pass or fail the placement tests. The scores are for information only. As I have indicated earlier, it is quite common these days to think of the scores as useful indicators but *not* a mandatory basis for making decisions.

Having said this, it is probably best in the vast majority of cases to take placement tests results seriously. If you have deficiencies, you will be advised to take basic courses that prepare you for more demanding work. Students often seek to avoid these courses, which have slang labels such as "bonehead." As in building a home, however, it is a good idea to lay a solid foundation before putting up the framing. Similarly, it is a good idea to make sure that your reading, English, and mathematical skills are solid before you try to climb the higher rungs of academic achievement.

GETTING FAMILIAR WITH GRADUATION REQUIREMENTS

Assuming that your long-term goal is a four-year degree, you will usually be advised to take your basic graduation requirements in your first two years of academic work. In your last two years you can take mainly courses in your major with room for a few electives. Electives are optional courses that are not required but that may fulfill a personal interest.

The kinds of courses that satisfy graduation requirements are known as *general education* or *breadth education* courses. The idea is to make you somewhat conversant with the spectrum of human knowledge. Usually these courses fall into broad categories such as social sciences, humanities, natural sciences, physical sciences, mathematics, foreign languages, applied arts, and health education. Within these categories you can usually make, within limits, your own selections. I say *within limits* because it is usually wise to take, even in the case of general education courses, those that deal in some way with your major.

Some students have an attitude problem toward general education courses. Frequently they think something like, "I want to be an accountant. I don't want to be sitting here in this philosophy course learning about Aristotle." Reflect on this attitude for a moment: It is very limited and uninformed. Although the teachings of Aristotle do not impinge directly upon the subject of accounting, they do so *indirectly*. For example, Aristotle was an insightful student of human nature. An accountant in private practice who wants to build a large clientele will do far better than others in the profession if he or she understands the needs and emotions of clients.

The assumption that colleges make by requiring a wide range of general courses is that you will become not merely a specialist but also an *educated person*. And the larger assumption is that an educated person makes a better specialist. A related assumption in all of this is that *all* subjects are connected to each other in a complex network. Consequently, they all support and enhance one another.

The best advice is that you should relax and develop a positive attitude toward general education requirements.

Study the graduation requirements of your college carefully. Know what you are taking and why. Although I have defended the educational philosophy underlying graduation requirements, it is equally true that it is folly to go down a lot of blind alleys taking courses that overlap and that have little or nothing to do with your major. I have seen students take a whole year of extra academic work because they were befuddled about graduation requirements.

CONCLUDING REMARKS

In this chapter, I have provided basic information that shows you how to gain admission to a college. Actually, it is really not too hard to get into college. Many colleges, particularly community colleges, have an open-door policy. And, as indicated in Chapter 2, a number of four-year institutions have alternative admissions programs.

It has been jokingly said, however, that "the open door often becomes a revolving door." And, unfortunately, there is some truth to the quip. The student gets in, encounters difficulties, drops out, and feels helpless and demoralized. Consequently, the subject of *staying in* is the focus of the next chapter. And, in a larger sense, the remainder of this book is about staying in, *and succeeding in*, college.

KEY POINTS TO REMEMBER

- The first important person to contact at a college is a counselor in the Counseling Office.
- If you are a part-time student, it is a good idea to sign up for no more than two or three courses the first semester you return to school.
- A well-defined academic major makes it easier to determine what classes to take. On the other hand, you may have to spend a semester or two discovering your interests and your ultimate vocational direction.
- Formal admission can be made at the Admissions Office. You will be given forms to fill out. Also, you will be asked to pay fees and provide a high school transcript.
- You may have to wait in line to register. And you may run into closed classes. Both of these problems can often be overcome in the future by making sure you register early.
- It is important to become oriented in college. You need to know your way around the campus, including the services that are available to you. And you need to know the conditions set forth in the college catalog.
- Placement tests fall into a general category of testing known as *educational testing*. The goal of placement tests is to measure your skill level, or how well you can perform, in three critical areas: reading, English, and mathematics.

- If you are applying for a highly selective college, a placement test result may be used as a screening device.
- If you have already been admitted to a college, a placement test result is usually used primarily for advice and guidance.
- The kinds of courses that satisfy graduation requirements are known as *general education* or *breadth education* courses. The aim of such courses is to help you become not merely a specialist, but also an *educated person*. Students sometimes take too many courses because they are befuddled about graduation requirements.

4

STAYING IN

A Survey of Student Support Services

Now that you have been admitted to college, have taken placement tests, and are enrolled for classes, a key issue becomes *staying in.* The overall college dropout rate is discouraging—probably no more than one-half of people who attend college ever earn a four-year degree. In the case of community colleges, attrition is very high. It is commonplace to lose from the rolls 30 to 40 percent of students in a given class.

Statistics can be discouraging, but as Benjamin Disraeli said, "There are lies, damned lies, and statistics." The positive side of the statistics can be seen. Approximately one-half of people who attend college *do* earn a four-year degree. Sixty to 70 percent of students who enroll for a class pass it and earn credit for it.

The truth of the matter is that you are a person, an individual, not a statistic. The humanistic viewpoint in psychology asserts that you have consciousness and will, and you can use these faculties to go against the odds. The psychologist Alfred Adler, one of the founding figures in early psychoanalysis, spoke of the Creative Self, a force within us that gives us freedom of choice and the capacity to write the script for our own personal fate. You can write a winning script.

The college is on your side, because it wants you to succeed. No college is happy with a high student dropout rate. This chapter presents a survey of student support services, services designed to help you stay in college. The rest of the book details what you can do for yourself to become an effective student.

THE HIGH-RISK STUDENT

The concept of the high-risk student has arisen in educational circles because of the high dropout rate. A *high-risk student* is one who is more likely than most to drop out of college. Such a student is said to be *vulnerable*, meaning he or she has either academic weaknesses or personal problems that contribute to feelings of discouragement and helplessness. The aim of student support services is to offset academic weaknesses or personal problems and to help the student feel both effective and hopeful.

There is, of course, no such thing as the typical high-risk student. There are, instead, high-risk students with a spectrum of problems and differences. Having said this, however, certain specific traits or characteristics do tend to be evident among high-risk students. The traits are not mutually exclusive. They overlap, and a student may display more than one. Here are some of the key characteristics associated with high-risk students:

1. *A lack of financial resources.* There just doesn't seem to be enough money to go around — to pay the rent, to have a minimal social life, to buy textbooks, and so forth. It is difficult to go on when one can barely find enough money to cover expenses.

2. *Job conflicts.* An adult in college often has to work 25 to 40 hours a week at outside employment. A recent retention-study committee at my college conducted a study of the reasons why students drop out of college. It developed that the most common single reason was job conflicts. A student will sign up for a group of classes and have an ideal schedule in terms of work. But the semester is more than four months long, and during that time the employer may want to change the student's hours or the student changes jobs. In a conflict situation, the job often wins.

3. *Academic underpreparation.* Many students who attempt college work are deficient in reading, English, and mathematical skills. This is not a sign of low intelligence, or a sign of inability to learn, but it

is a sign that for some reason in the student's learning history basic skills were not acquired to a sufficient level of competence. Perhaps grammar school and high school instruction were poor. Perhaps the student went to overcrowded schools. Perhaps the parents were irresponsible and abusive. Perhaps the student had a negative attitude in high school. All of these, and more, are distinct possibilities. But the past is past and the student can still become an effective learner in the present.

4. *Learning disabilities.* A learning disability may sound the same as Item 3, but it is not. A *learning disability* exists when there is a sensory problem, or sometimes a muscle control problem, that interferes with a student's capacity to learn. The two most common general categories of learning disabilities are impairments of vision or hearing.

5. *An absence of academic direction.* The student has a desire for higher education but cannot define an educational goal. Consequently, the student wanders in circles, taking this course or that, and wastes time. Discouraged, this student may eventually drop out of the system entirely.

6. *Responsibilities toward children.* If a student has children who are under five or six years of age, who are not yet enrolled for full-time programs in grammar school, there is the problem of competent day care. The parent who is worried about the safety and welfare of children has a hard time concentrating on studies.

7. *Personal problems.* It is fairly common for a student to be going through a life crisis. Troubled relationships with the opposite sex, including marriage problems, are a frequent source of distress. Sometimes a student abuses alcohol or other drugs. A student may suffer from mental and emotional problems, including suicidal tendencies, depression, and chronic anxiety.

8. *A negative self-concept as a student.* Many students see themselves as incompetent and ineffective learners. Some of these students avoid difficult classes and set their academic level of aspiration far below their real abilities. Conversely, some of these students put up a false front, sign up for very difficult classes, and set their academic level of aspiration unrealistically high. When they fail and drop out, they avoid psychological failure by criticizing the educational system.

REVISITING THE COUNSELING OFFICE

If you suspect that you are a high-risk student, you should revisit the Counseling Office. Your counselor will be able to direct you toward one of the other campus offices representing the kind of student support service that will help you stay in college. Frequently, you will be given a booklet that details the various campus student support services. In most cases a telephone number and the name of a person to contact will be provided.

If you have been admitted to a college, the college wants you to stay in. The college aims to help you, and behind the scenes administrators and various faculty committees are working to establish ways to encourage and retain students.

If you have a lack of academic direction, you are already in the right place. Your counselor can arrange for you to take standardized tests that will help you decide on an academic major and eventual vocation. The two basic kinds of tests that are helpful are aptitude and interest tests. An aptitude test evaluates the capacity to acquire the skills required in a given vocational area. Examples of the kinds of aptitudes evaluated are mechanical, clerical, artistic, musical, verbal reasoning, numerical ability, and abstract reasoning.

An *interest* test evaluates the *preference* that a student displays for one career field over another. Examples of interest areas include nature, adventure, military activities, mathematics, medical science, law, social service, athletics, domestic arts, agriculture, and teaching.

Aptitude and interest tests do not impose anything on you. The tests results are an organized psychological map of what you may experience as a seething cauldron of wishes and ambitions. The tests bring some order to chaos. After the tests are scored, you can discuss the results with your counselor. It is up to you to decide how to use the results. Often, they will help you develop a strong sense of academic direction.

If you have a personal problem, the Counseling Office is also the right place to go. A counselor will often have either a Master's degree or a Ph.D. in counseling psychology. Such an individual is qualified to do more than academic counseling. The trained counselor can help you to evaluate difficult choices you must make in a personal crisis situation, find ways to communicate more effectively with a partner or children, clarify your thinking processes, and improve your self-esteem. However, counseling is *not* psychotherapy. If you are a deeply troubled person, and if you have mental and emotional problems that need treatment, this is beyond the scope of counseling. In a case like this the counselor usually has available a list of community resources and can make a referral to an agency, clinic, or therapist in private practice.

THE ADULT REENTRY CENTER

Not every college has an adult reentry center. With more and more adults reentering college, however, adult reentry centers are becoming quite common. The functions of the Adult Reentry Center overlap with the functions of the Counseling Office. And the center is usually staffed by individuals with the same general kind of training.

What is adult reentry? The concept of *adult reentry* implies that the adult is reentering any kind of school, including college. This may be the adult's first college experience. The concept of reentry suggests that there has been a distinct break in the individual's academic education. He or she has been out of school for four or five years or more. There are frequently family responsibilities, job conflicts, and special financial needs. The reentry adult often wonders if it is possible to come back to school at all. The main function of the Adult Reentry Center is to provide counseling and guidance that makes returning to school *really possible.*

A good adult reentry center helps returning students feel welcome; it assists them in getting over the feeling that they are strangers on the campus, that they are outsiders, that they don't belong back in school. Many of the same services available in the Counseling Center are offered, but they are given the special focus required by the reentering adult.

Sometimes the Adult Reentry Center organizes support groups for reentering students. In small-group discussions students can meet others with similar problems, discuss attitudes toward school, and receive encouragement.

The Adult Reentry Center may also offer short, optional classes in assertiveness training, stress reduction, behavior modification with children, and weight control. All of these classes are designed to enhance personal effectiveness and self-esteem. The reasoning is that many reentry students are assailed with doubts. They question their own abilities excessively. They see themselves, as Chapter 1 indicated, as adults in a college full of kids. They think, incorrectly, that the "kids" are competent learners and that they are not. The reentry student needs to rediscover lost strengths and realize that he or she has a great deal of untapped potential. Various studies have shown that the reentry student is a high-risk student, a student overly likely to drop out of the system. The Adult Reentry Center exists to prevent this from happening.

If your college has an adult reentry center, be sure to visit it and find out what services it offers to students like you.

FINANCIAL AID

The college you go to will almost certainly have a Financial Aid Office. Financial aid to students is a big subject, and it requires an expert to inform a student correctly about scholarships, loans, and grants. Consequently, your college will have a Financial Aid Officer, an individual trained in helping students who need financial aid. He or she will be able to provide you with accurate, up-to-date information.

As indicated above, financial aid tends to fall into three broad categories: scholarships, loans, and grants. *Scholarships* are sums of money that are given to students who have demonstrated above-average academic ability. The money does not have to be repaid. The idea is to encourage excellence and competence in learning. Some scholarships are based on financial need and some are not. Students often have the idea that they have to be straight-A students in order to be eligible for a scholarship. Consequently, many never apply. The truth is that many scholarships, both small and large, are often available in special categories, and you may very well qualify *if you apply*. It *is* true, however, that you need an academic track record and letters of recommendation from instructors. So it generally doesn't make sense for a reentering student to apply for a scholarship of any kind until approximately a semester of academic work has been completed.

Loans are sums of money that have to be repaid with interest. They represent borrowed money, and consequently they will be a long-term responsibility. The two basic kinds of loans available to students are private loans and government loans. *Private loans* are provided through banks and other commercial lending agencies. Student loans provided by these organizations usually have relatively low interest rates in contrast to their other loans. Also, students may be given favorable conditions for qualification. *Government loans* are provided primarily by the federal government, the state, or a combination of both. These loans, like all loans, must be repaid with interest. However, the interest rates are lower than those available through commercial organizations. Also, it is extremely easy to qualify for these loans. In fact, they are made readily available to students who would not otherwise be able to borrow money. Usually government loans do not have to be repaid until you have completed your higher education. And there is, in addition, a grace period. Because of a liberal government loan program, it is possible for many students to go to college.

A *grant* is a sum of money that does not have to be repaid. It is in essence a gift. The U.S. Department of Education has developed a plan that requires state participation. At the federal level the plan is known as the *State Student Incentive Grant Program*. Your state has a specific name for its program, and the Financial Aid Administrator will know about it. Grants, unlike scholarships, are not based primarily on academic ability. They are based on financial need. You have to apply to find out if you qualify.

The Financial Aid Office will have available a free government booklet entitled *The Student Guide: Financial Aid From the U.S. Department of Education.* Obtain a copy of this booklet and get familiar with its provisions. Also, do not hesitate to ask questions of the Financial Aid Officer, as he or she is qualified to counsel you.

THE ACADEMIC ADVISER

The academic adviser is somewhat different from the general counselor in the Counseling Office. An *academic adviser* is an instructor who teaches a specific subject such as history, English, biology, or accounting. Once you have decided on an academic major you will be assigned an academic adviser. Instead of general counseling you can now obtain specific advice on courses to take for your major. If you are in a community college, the academic adviser can provide transfer information and recommend colleges where you can complete your four-year degree. Also, the academic adviser will have information about careers in your major. Although academic advisers are primarily instructors, not counselors, they are usually required by their contracts to keep regular, posted hours when they are available for advice.

The academic adviser may have had career experience in a vocational area outside of the classroom. For example, in my own case I give advice to psychology majors. I have worked in a mental hospital in the Air Force, at a state mental hospital, and in private practice. I am also the author of several textbooks and popular books in psychology. When I advise students, I find out something about their dreams, abilities, and life situations, and usually I can give the student effective career guidance.

My kind of general vocational experience is not unusual. One of my colleagues teaches administration of justice and advises students majoring in both law and law enforcement. She has been a police officer and probation counselor, and she has a law degree. Another colleague teaches accounting and real estate and advises students majoring in both of these areas. He has worked as an accountant for several organizations, has sold real estate, and works part time as a real estate appraiser.

It is obvious that almost any college faculty member is a gold mine of information. You just have to know how to tap the mine. The basic approach is simply to make appointments and ask questions.

You do not have to wait to be assigned an adviser. If you take a class in your major from an instructor that you perceive as informed and helpful, you can approach that individual directly for advice. You can request from the person that he or she be your adviser, and in most cases the instructor will agree.

DAY CARE

Many colleges have day-care facilities for toddlers and preschoolers who are aged approximately two to six. Toddlers have to be toilet-trained and capable of some self-control to be accepted. Seldom are the day-care facilities adequate to handle infants. In many cases the day-care facility will be state-supported, and no charge, or a modest one, will be made for its services. It is common for colleges to offer full-time day care, including snacks and a meal at lunchtime. A good day-care facility is fenced and secure, and both play and educational facilities should be provided.

More often than not a college day-care facility is under the supervision of a person with a degree in early childhood development. Parents are frequently asked to volunteer two or three hours a week in order to staff the facility and keep costs down. Frequently the day-care center offers free classes in communication skills and behavior modification with children. If you are a parent with young children, the existence of a day-care center on a college campus may make the difference between becoming or not becoming a student.

TUTORIAL SERVICE

Many colleges have a Learning Center, a facility that provides tutoring and skills courses. Usually the Learning Center is headed by a full-time director who has had training in helping students who have academic problems. Tutors are available on a one-to-one basis without charge. They are students who have already succeeded in a given course. For example, if you need tutoring in biology, your tutor will be a fellow student who has earned an A or a B in biology. A good tutor will encourage you, explain difficult concepts, and help you get organized in a class.

The tutor is a part-time student worker and is paid an hourly rate for student workers. If you become an effective student, you might eventually find yourself tutoring as a source of extra income. Tutoring is itself a learning process, and it is good training if you are planning to become a teacher yourself.

Effective tutoring can often make the difference between a whole point in the final grade. A student who would have otherwise earned an F or D may earn a C. A student who would have otherwise earned a C may do B work or better. Tutoring is an ancient tradition in education. For example, the Roman elite used tutors two thousand years ago to educate their children, and the philosopher Aristotle was tutor to Alexander the Great. You can take advantage of this old, and still useful, method of education.

CLASSES IN READING AND OTHER SKILLS

Almost everyone has heard of the three Rs: readin', 'riting, and 'rithmetic. This old formula has it just about right. The three basic-skills areas assessed for college work are reading, English, and mathematics, as was discussed earlier. If your placement tests show that you have deficiencies in a basic skill, your counselor will recommend that you take remedial courses offered by the Learning Center.

Many students stay away from remedial courses. They know they *should* take them, but they have two problems. First, they are embarrassed to take the courses. They feel that they are being laughed at, that taking a remedial course is a sign of failure. Second, remedial courses usually do not carry credit toward a four-year degree. Consequently, students think they are wasting time.

Let's do a little realistic thinking, however. A *remedial course* is, by definition, one that offers a "remedy." And a *remedy* is that which cures or corrects an error. Consequently, the *aim* of a remedial course is to overcome a deficiency in a basic skills area. The student who needs remediation, and who has a positive attitude toward it, will generally fare much better in the long run than the student who avoids remedial courses. The courses are taught by credentialed teachers with special training in remediation. These teachers are usually nurturing and student oriented. They work diligently to give the student basic skills and the confidence to forge ahead and succeed.

For example, Paige E. dropped out of high school at 16. She was pregnant and married her boyfriend. At age 27 she had two children and was divorced. She applied for admission to the local community college, where her placement tests showed that she needed remediation primarily in reading and English. She took the recommended remedial courses and had a positive attitude toward them. Today, ten years later, she has a Ph.D. in educational psychology and is a full-time contract instructor at a state college. One of her principal interests is in the learning process and its application to remedial work.

If you need help to improve your skills in reading, English, or mathematics, don't hesitate to take advantage of remedial courses.

LEARNING DISABILITY SERVICES

As indicated earlier, a *learning disability* exists when there is a sensory problem, or sometimes a muscle-control problem, that interferes with a student's capacity to learn. The two most common general categories of learning disabilities are impairments of vision or hearing. A learning disability, in contrast to low scores in a skill area, is thought of as essentially a physical handicap.

Dyslexia, also called *developmental reading disorder*, usually has roots in childhood. Its key trait is difficulty in learning to read with proficiency. The adult with dyslexia will find it difficult to read aloud with fluency, will often reverse the order of letters, and will not recognize certain words. Another, more obvious visual impairment, is blindness or partial blindness.

Some children and adults suffer from a disorder known as *dysgraphia*, an impairment in the ability to write. For example, they can write only in large, crude block letters. Or, for a second example, their writing is so tiny and crabbed that it is illegible to most readers.

Deafness, partial deafness, or the inability to hear certain pitches are examples of hearing impairments. Students with a hearing impairment are often encouraged to tape-record lectures. The information on the tape can be transcribed by a friend or secretarial service and studied at a later date.

The Learning Disabilities Center has trained specialists who work with impaired students. They provide advice and services that make it possible to succeed in class. For example, a learning disability specialist might read a test and mark the answer sheet on a one-to-one basis for a student with a visual impairment. This is usually done privately on an appointment basis in the Learning Disabilities Center.

CONCLUDING REMARKS

The main aim of this chapter is to convince you that once a college admits you as a student, *it wants you to succeed.* As you can see from the information provided, a substantial array of student support services has been arranged for your benefit. Administrators, instructors, and counselors spend many hours working in committees that exist to increase the effectiveness of student support services.

Unfortunately, student support services tend to be underutilized. Many students are shy and intimidated by clerks and administrators. And it is true that on occasion a particular clerk or a particular administrator may be cold and lack interest in you as a person. However, these kinds of people are the exception, not the rule. Even under adverse circumstances, you need to stand your ground, be assertive, and obtain the service you need.

Don't hesitate to take advantage of student support services. They can help you stay in college and achieve your long-term academic goals.

KEY POINTS TO REMEMBER

- *Student support services* are services designed to help you stay in college.
- A *high-risk student* is one who is more likely than most to drop out of college. Such a student is said to be *vulnerable.*
- The chapter identified eight key characteristics of high-risk students. The chapter also demonstrated ways that negative characteristics can often be offset by student support services.
- If you suspect that you are a high-risk student, you will want to revisit the Counseling Office and obtain information on student support services.
- The main function of the Adult Reentry Center is to provide counseling and guidance that makes returning to school *really possible.*
- Financial aid tends to fall into three broad categories: scholarships, loans, and grants.
- An *academic adviser* is an instructor who teaches a specific subject such as history, English, biology, or accounting. The academic counselor is qualified to give you specific advice on your academic major.

- Many colleges have day-care facilities for toddlers and preschoolers.
- The Learning Center often provides tutors on a one-to-one basis without charge.
- The Learning Center also offers remedial courses in basic-skills areas such as reading, English, and mathematics.
- A *learning disability* exists when there is a sensory problem, or sometimes a muscle-control problem, that interferes with a student's ability to learn. The Learning Disabilities Center has trained specialists who work with impaired students.

5

HOW TO CONCENTRATE ON A TEXTBOOK

*A Sure-Fire Way to Earn
High Grades*

The following is an excerpt from the personal journal of Anna W., a 31-year-old mother of three children ranging in age from 5 to 11:

> I've just spent a couple of hours off and on reading Chapter 2 in my philosophy textbook. There's supposed to be a test on it tomorrow and I only have a vague idea of what I have read. It's as if my mind is a mirror. The words and ideas are reflected in it, and they seem clear enough at the moment, but when I go to the next paragraph or page, there seems to be no permanent impression left. And that's during good phases! Half the time I find my mind drifting off the subject — I'm worrying about the kids or being interrupted by them. Or I'm thinking about what I have to cook for dinner or a phone call I have to make. Sometimes I realize I have sort of read a half of a page like a robot — and I wake up to the fact that I'm just going through a kind of meaningless motion. I really don't know what to do. With my responsibilities and the demands on my time I don't know if I'll ever be able to concentrate on a textbook. If I can't find a better way, I'll have to quit school.

Anna is not alone. Many people, including me, simply can't concentrate on a textbook for a sustained period of time. And even if you do feel you are focusing on the material, there is the problem of retention. How do you know you are prepared for an examination? Has the information stuck? Can you recall it, reproduce it, or recognize it? When we read a magazine article, a novel, or a newspaper editorial we do not expect to be tested on it. So what we retain is a matter of chance and personal interest. And it is our own business. In the case of a textbook, the subject matter is assigned and personal interest may be high or low. Also, we *will* be tested. In brief, there is an enormous amount of difference between *reading* and *studying*. This is a distinction that many students don't really make. They believe that they have done their duty if they have read an assignment.

This chapter will show you how to concentrate—with the greatest of ease—on any textbook. And it will show you how to retain what you study.

THE NATURE OF HUMAN ATTENTION

Before we proceed to specific methods, it will be helpful for you to become more familiar with the nature of human attention. *Attention* is a process by which we concentrate our consciousness on a narrow range of available sensory or mental information. For example, if you are absorbed in working a crossword puzzle, you may not notice immediately that someone else has entered the room. Or, if you are daydreaming and preoccupied with a personal fantasy, you may tune out a professor and retain very little information from a lecture.

Attention is an important aspect of the learning process because we learn through our senses. It requires vision, hearing, taste, touch, or smell in order to have the kind of experiences that result in learning. And a sense has to *focus* on the information coming to it before the data can enter your mind or be learned.

William James, one of the founders of American psychology, made a distinction between voluntary attention and involuntary attention. *Voluntary attention* is the kind of attention in which you focus on information by an act of will. You tell yourself, "I will give this my time and my thought," or, "I have to read this for a test," or "I had better listen to what the boss is saying." Voluntary attention is a matter of choice. Nothing compelling or interesting about the information commands the attention. Paying attention is a kind of good will gesture on our part. Consequently, no matter how honorable our intentions are, there is a strong tendency for attention to drift away from its target. Soon we find we are paying attention to something unintended, and we don't even know how it happened.

Involuntary attention is the kind of attention in which you focus on information automatically without a conscious effort. It is the kind of attention being described in the last line of the preceding paragraph. Involuntary attention is always more intense and absorbing than voluntary attention. It is freely given, spontaneous, reflexive, and unforced. James noted that some sources of stimulation have what he called "a directly exciting quality." As examples he listed strange things, moving things, wild animals, bright things, pretty things, metallic things, blows, and blood. He pointed out that if a stimulus is intense or sudden we tend to pay attention to it. For example, we automatically pay attention when a telephone rings.

On a more formal level, the two factors that appear to control involuntary attention are change of stimulation and motivation. *Change of stimulation* refers to the fact that lights, sounds, and other energy sources in the environment vary, sometimes suddenly, in intensity and quality. If a light that has been burning steadily blinks, we notice it. If a light changes its color we notice it. If a television commercial suddenly seems to increase in loudness, we notice it. We also notice shifts *downward* in intensity. For example, if you have been a sleeping passenger in a car, you are likely to wake up when the car stops its motion. The key word that ties all of this together is *novelty*. We pay attention when there is an element of novelty in the environment.

The other factor that controls involuntary attention is *motivation*. We attend to information that helps us meet a biological or emotional need. If you are on a long drive and are hungry, you will automatically begin to notice restaurant signs. If you feel somewhat deprived of love and romance, you will find it easy to concentrate on the dialogue and action in a novel revolving around these subjects.

It would be a student's paradise if the textbooks assigned could elicit our involuntary attention. Unfortunately, they do not. In the majority of cases, even if you have some degree of interest in a subject you are studying, you will find that you will have to give forced attention to a textbook. It's unfortunate, but it's just a fact of life. Even if the author includes anecdotes and pictures with interesting captions, there's something about the fact that a textbook is just that, a textbook, that makes it lose some of its natural appeal. We know we have to read everything assigned. We know we will be tested. We feel somewhat threatened. All of these factors, and more, conspire to make it difficult to attend to textbooks the way we attend to novels and popular nonfiction books.

Consequently, you need a way to trick your attention into working the way you want it to. And that is where a study method enters the picture. A *study method* is an organized approach that allows the student to attend without effort, learn easily, retain what is learned, and be able to reproduce or recognize the learned information on an examination. Let us turn to a well-researched, master study method.

THE TRIED-AND-TRUE SQ3R METHOD

In the late 1940s the research psychologist Francis P. Robinson conducted a large-scale research project designed to diagnose and deal with the academic difficulties of students. One of the important outcomes of Robinson's work was the SQ3R study method. With almost 50 years of experience behind it, the method stands out as perhaps the most logical and useful study method ever devised. Various investigations suggest that if a student uses the method correctly, it can easily make the difference of at least a whole rank in a projected course grade. A student who might have earned a D in a class will move up to a C. Another student who might have earned a B in a class is likely to earn an A instead.

The method works. You would think that it would be taught in every grammar school and high school in the United States, but interestingly enough very few students have even heard of it. When I ask an introductory psychology class of about 40 students if they are familiar with the method, usually only about four or five hands go up. It appears that approximately 90 percent of entering college students of any age don't know about the method.

It is important that you know about the method. And it is even more important that you *use* it.

SQ3R stands for *survey, question, read, recite,* and *review.* I will describe each step in the method in practical terms.

Survey

Let's say that you have been assigned a chapter to study in a particular textbook. The method can be readily applied to almost any subject. First you survey the chapter. Flip slowly through the pages looking at headings, subheadings, terms in boldface, definitions in italics, captions under photographs, tables, charts, and figures. Read quickly the summary at the end of the chapter, without any effort to retain its contents. The survey will not take you long. Ten to 15 minutes is a typical length of time.

A first purpose of the survey is to give you what psychologists call a Gestalt. *Gestalt* is a German word and is generally translated as an organized whole, a pattern, or a configuration. In this case, getting the Gestalt means that you obtain the grand picture of the chapter. And this makes it easier for you to make sense of the chapter's various "parts" or details. You will more readily see where they fit in if you make the survey than if you start to study in detail on page 1.

A second purpose is to prepare your mind for information. In learning theory this is called *stimulus predifferentiation.* It is a process comparable to plowing a field before planting seeds. The survey prepares you to learn and retain information.

Question

From the beginning of the chapter, proceed by paragraphs. Skim each paragraph for its potential to generate a question. The headings, subheadings, terms in boldface, and definitions in italics referred to earlier are all likely sources for questions. Also, captions under photographs, tables, charts, and figures, also referred to earlier, provide sources for questions.

Look only for key concepts and important points. These are what will inspire the actual test questions that will be asked eventually by your professor. Students often doubt this. They sometimes think that teachers write questions from obscure footnotes or asides in parentheses. This is an illusion created by lack of adequate preparation. For example, I have often had a student complain that there was nothing about classical conditioning in a textbook. They are surprised when I point out a page of material on the subject. They missed the material through inattention because they were not using an active study method such as the one being described here. Be assured that if you cover the key concepts and important points you will have touched on 90 percent or more of what can be asked on a test.

Here are some examples of the kinds of questions you can generate. They are drawn from different textbooks on different subjects.

1. What is the doctrine of Manifest Destiny? (history)
2. What are DNA and RNA? (biology)
3. What is a light year? (astronomy)
4. How does the doctrine of voluntarism differ from the doctrine of determinism? (philosophy)
5. According to B. F. Skinner, what is operant conditioning? (psychology)
6. How does a trust deed secure a note? (real estate principles)
7. What is the electromagnetic spectrum? (physics)

For a basic grasp of concepts, questions that generally begin with the words "What is . . ." are the best. Such questions strike at the heart of the concept. The eventual answer tends to illuminate the concept and reveal it in sharp relief.

How many questions should you ask for a given chapter? This depends on the density of the information. Some books give lengthy examples and anecdotes. These exist only to make a concept meaningful and are not a source of questions in and of themselves. Other books will have a high density of information with as many as three or four important points on a page. (This is particularly true of science books.) If a chapter has 20 pages you may find yourself writing 70 or 80 questions. Don't be dismayed! When you actually use the SQ3R method, you will find that the writing and the answering of the questions is a more rapid procedure than you might expect.

Read

Go back to question 1 and read for its answer. When you are satisfied that you know the answer, summarize it in writing in one or two sentences. If a definition is involved, it is all right to copy it verbatim. But be sure that you are satisfied that you know what the definition means.

Definitions usually involve a term and its related concept. In order to make concepts clear, it is usually essential to have at least one good example. If the book provides an example, and it almost certainly will, again summarize it *in writing* in one or two sentences. As an exercise, see if you can generalize the concept. Try to think of an example of your own, although it is not necessary to write this out.

If a typewriter or word processor is available, the above process will be greatly facilitated. Avoid the temptation to overwrite. An answer should be no more than two to five sentences, including a definition and example.

Proceed to questions 2, 3, and so forth.

Here are some model answers to three of the questions asked in the previous section:

Question 1. What is the doctrine of Manifest Destiny?

Answer. A doctrine used by the U.S. government to provide a superficially plausible rationale for its westward expansion. President James K. Polk invoked the doctrine when he annexed Texas in a struggle with Mexico.

Question 3. What is a light year?

Answer. The distance that light can travel in one year. The speed of light is approximately 186,000 miles per second. So a light year is about 6,000,000,000,000 (six trillion) miles.

Question 5. According to B. F. Skinner, what is operant conditioning?

Answer. According to B. F. Skinner, one of the leading behaviorists of the twentieth century, operant conditioning is a learning process in which an action produces a consequence or reinforcer. An animal example is provided by a rat pressing a lever to obtain food. A human example is provided by a professor telling a joke to obtain the attention of a class.

Recite

When you have a complete list of questions and answers for a chapter, it is time to recite the answers. Go back to question 1 and cover up its answer. Now try to recite the answer as best you can. Recitation is a fairly demanding task because it requires both the recall and the reproduction of information.

The satisfactory recitation of an answer can take more than one form. You can memorize the answer and recite it word for word. This is tempting, and there is really nothing wrong with this as long as you are sure that you *understand* what you are saying. It is not essential to memorize, however. If you can paraphrase the answer and recite its gist, or substance, this is fine. The capacity to formulate an answer in your own words reveals that you have some mastery of the information.

There are several ways to recite answers. You can write them out, but this is time consuming and perhaps overly tedious in view of the fact that you have already written the answers. You can recite mentally, running the answers in sentences through your conscious mind. This is probably the way most of us will use the SQ3R method. It has the drawback of being somewhat passive, however, and you may be kidding yourself that you know something when you don't. Consequently, at least some of the time you should do some oral recitation. Say the answers in normal tones if you are alone or in a soft voice if others are within hearing range.

Compare recitation to rehearsals for a play. The actors engage in a number of rehearsals before they feel prepared for a performance. The same logic applies here. An examination is the student's equivalent of the actor's performance.

Studies by educational psychologists and learning theorists suggest that recitation is one of the most important steps in the SQ3R method. Fully 50 percent of your study time should be spent in recitation. Unfortunately, it is a step that many students slight or never take. Active recitation of answers is really the master key that opens the twin doors of learning and retention.

Review

When you can answer all of the questions your main work for a chapter is complete. During the evening or morning before an examination all that you have to do is invest a brief session in review. Double-check to make sure that you can respond to every question. If there are a few that are still giving you difficulty, give more time to these. The time that other students spend in cramming in a state of panic you will be spending in confident review.

VARIATIONS ON THE SQ3R METHOD

You should think of the SQ3R method in its traditional form as your primary study method. It is, of course, possible to impose all sorts of modifications on the method in accordance with your own personality, time constraints, and personal preferences.

One method is to combine the SQ3R method with the use of flash cards. Put each question on the front of a 3"-by-5" index card. The answer is placed on the back of the card. One advantage of the cards is that you can use them to avoid unwanted sequential learning effects. *Sequential learning effects* take place when a response is triggered not by a question but by the fact that a certain answer is in a certain position (e.g., answer 4). A common example of sequential learning is the capacity to recite the alphabet. We say "D" after "C" because of its position. You can shuffle the cards and take the questions at random, consequently breaking down sequential learning effects.

A second advantage of the cards is that you can give more attention to difficult questions. As you learn the material, set aside easy questions and give more of your study time to difficult ones.

Albert H., a 34-year-old grocery clerk and father who takes night classes, always takes 10 to 15 cards wrapped with a rubber band with him wherever he goes. When he is standing in a bank line, for example, he gives study time to the cards.

Another variation on the SQ3R method involves studying with someone else. If you are taking a class with a friend or an acquaintance you have made in the class, you can take turns asking each other the questions and reciting the answers. Also, you can divide up the task of writing questions and answers.

Beverly C., a 29-year-old suburban homemaker and mother of two children, spends a lot of time in a car taking her children to various places and running errands. She puts questions and answers on a cassette tape and then listens to the tape whenever she is driving alone. She says that hearing her own voice repeat the material helps her to learn.

CONCLUDING REMARKS

One of the common objections to the SQ3R method is, "It takes too much time. I'm busy and I don't have time to spare." It is certainly true that as an adult college student you have to manage your time effectively. However, the objection is without merit. In the long run the SQ3R method takes *less time* than passive reading because it is effective and you are using your time well.

You will find that in general the task of writing questions and answers goes rather rapidly. You tend to abstract key points, consequently not wasting your time on irrelevant and redundant information.

Also, the fact that you have made yourself into an active learner puts you on psychological alert. You are task-oriented. You have to scan actively for questions worth writing. And you have to think about the best way to frame an answer briefly. Both of these tasks automatically focus your attention. Consequently, you will concentrate on a textbook *automatically* without conscious effort. You have invoked what William James, referred to earlier, described as involuntary attention in contrast to voluntary attention. Assuming that you are a busy adult with interests and responsibilities other than your course work, you will find the capacity of the SQ3R method to induce this process of involuntary attention is a real blessing.

As the subtitle of this chapter indicates, the SQ3R method with its variations is a sure-fire way to earn high grades.

KEY POINTS TO REMEMBER

- There is an enormous amount of difference between *reading* and *studying*.
- *Attention* is a process by which we concentrate our consciousness on a narrow range of available sensory or mental information.
- According to William James, *voluntary attention* is the kind of attention in which you focus on information by an act of will. *Involuntary attention* is the kind of attention in which you focus on information automatically without conscious effort.

- A *study method* is an organized approach that allows the student to attend without effort, learn easily, retain what is learned, and be able to reproduce or recognize the learned information on an examination.
- The SQ3R method—standing for Survey, Question, Read, Recite, and Review—is a master study method.
- The principal purpose of a survey is to obtain an overview of a chapter, or block of material, to be studied.
- Questions should be made up by referring to headings, subheadings, terms in boldface, definitions in italics, captions under photographs, tables, charts, and figures. Look only for key concepts and important points.
- Read with the purpose of answering questions. Summarize the essence of the answer *in writing* using no more than one or two sentences. If an example is required, use no more than one or two additional sentences.
- Spend approximately 50 percent of your study time in actively reciting answers to questions.
- During the evening or morning before an examination, invest a brief session in a review of your list of questions and answers.
- An effective variation on the SQ3R method is to combine it with the use of flash cards.
- The SQ3R method helps you to use your time efficiently and effectively.

6

HOW PEOPLE LEARN

It Gets Easier

You are a learner.

We are all learners.

People learn all the time in all kinds of situations. We learn to walk. We learn to talk. We learn to swim, roller skate, and ride a bicycle. We learn our attitudes and the expectations of a family and a culture.

We may learn to despise a former friend. Conversely, a wife may tell a friend, "I don't think I really loved my husband on our wedding day. I married him for all the wrong reasons. But now, after five years of marriage, I have to say I have learned to love him."

Learning is an all-encompassing phenomenon. It doesn't take place only in an academic setting, in a school or a college. We cannot escape learning. The main questions of importance are: Are we effective learners? Are we learning what we are supposed to learn? These questions are of importance in all walks of life, including, of course, college.

At this point a definition of learning is needed. Here is a serviceable one: *Learning* is a more or less permanent change in behavior, or a behavioral tendency, as a result of experience. Notice that learning is "more or less" permanent because you can forget prior learning. Also, it can be extinguished or modified. Learning is not only a change in behavior, it is also a change in behavioral tendency, because learning is not always manifest. A distinction is made between *learning* and *performance*. For example, you may have learned the information for a test but because of anxiety or a personal problem you cannot perform well, and consequently you earn a low grade. Finally, the emphasis is on experience because we have to see and hear—watch and listen and pay attention—in order to learn.

Contrary to common belief, it does *not* get harder to learn as you get older and approach or reach middle age. You may have heard that people lose neurons, or brain cells, as they age. There is some truth in this statement, but the loss in a healthy person is relatively small in terms of percentages. And it is more than compensated for by the brain's huge capacity and its tendency to use elaborate back-up systems. Relax. Your age in and of itself is no handicap.

On the contrary, your age is a positive factor. The adult student has a wealth of background and associations to draw on, and this is an aid to the general learning process. Later on in this chapter, I will discuss a phenomenon called *learning to learn* that bears upon this theme.

My experience with hundreds of mature students suggests that on the whole they tend to be effective learners.

In view of the fact that the process of learning is so important, it is important to explore how people learn. This will help you learn in the most effective manner.

TAKING ADVANTAGE OF THE LAWS OF ASSOCIATION

The principal laws of association are (1) contiguity, (2) repetition, (3) attention, (4) pleasure-pain, and (5) similarity. The basic laws were formulated by Aristotle in approximately 300 B.C. and by John Locke in the seventeenth century. Both philosophers taught that the mind at birth is a blank slate and that all knowledge has to be acquired by learning. The laws they formulated still make up the backbone of modern learning theory. These are the same laws that are taught with flair and salesmanship in expensive memory training courses.

The law of *contiguity* states that the basic process of learning involves connecting two or more stimuli. Edward L. Thorndike was one of the first students of trial-and-error learning. In the early part of this century he said that "learning *is* connecting." The word contiguity means "touching" or "going together." We learn to associate stimuli that "touch" or "go together" in space and time. For example, what words have the most popular association with the words *thunder, bread,* and *mom*? The answers are likely to be *lightning, butter,* and *dad.* Notice that the associated pairs (e.g., thunder–lightning) actually go together in the real world. This is why we associate them.

Much of what you learn, even at a higher level such as college, involves contiguity and connecting. For example, you may be asked to learn a term and its definition. In a biology class you are taught that a *neuron* is a living cell that transmits information. In an astronomy class you are taught that a *light year* is the distance that light can travel in one year. Note that you can think of the term as element A and the definition as element B. You have to learn to connect the two elements. Seeing the term should suggest the definition, and seeing the definition should suggest the term. In this way you thus build a vocabulary. One good way to look at the subject matter in any course you take is in terms of the connections you are being asked to make.

The law of *repetition* says that we tend to learn stimuli that are presented more than once. Imagine that you live on an alien planet that has a storm only once every 50 years. If you experienced thunder and lightning that infrequently, you might never associate the two. In contrast, imagine that you live in the Yukon and you experience bad weather often. Thunder and lightning are welded together in your mind.

You can take advantage of the law of repetition. When you learned the multiplication tables in grammar school, you had to use repetition. The same principle is still true in college. You have to go over terms, definitions, facts, concepts, and examples more than once, perhaps several times, before you can make them your own.

The law of *attention* says that we do not learn unless we are actively taking note of stimuli. If you are daydreaming during a lecture, you will learn little or nothing. If your mind wanders when you are reading a textbook, you can "read" a whole page and next to nothing will register. Consequently, you need to be *active* when you are learning, and this will help you pay attention. The most practical thing to do during a lecture is to decide to take notes and write down the key points. This will keep you on alert and make you vigilant. You will be actively *deciding* what is worth noting and what is not. Similarly, when you study a textbook, you can take notes on it. Or you can use the SQ3R method detailed in Chapter 5.

The law of *pleasure-pain* states that we tend to learn that which brings us pleasure and avoid learning that which brings us pain. This principle resides at the root of animal training. A dog may learn to jump through a hoop because it receives a bit of dog candy after it does so. A tiger may avoid clawing its trainer because it is whipped when it makes a menacing move.

The pleasure-pain principle often makes students take the path of least resistance. For example, Katherine R. is taking four classes: creative writing, painting, algebra, and history. She is earning A's in creative writing and painting, but she is earning D's in algebra and history. The first two courses bring her pleasure whereas the second two are sources of psychological pain. She can spend hours writing a story, but she can only spend a few minutes at a time studying history. What should she do? After all, she *does* need to pass basic general education courses in order to graduate.

One strategy is to define learning in terms of relatively modest units of learning such as five pages, 10 terms, and so forth. Katherine can promise herself that *immediately* following the study of the unit she will give herself a small reward (i.e., pleasure). For example, she can read an interesting novel for 10 minutes, she can call a friend on the phone, she can watch television, or she can have a snack. The keys to using pleasure in this way are to provide yourself with the pleasure only *after* you have completed the self-imposed task and to keep the reward relatively small.

The law of *similarity* says we tend to learn a new stimulus fairly readily if it is somewhat like an already learned stimulus. For example, let's say that you are taking a class in child development and the instructor says, "When children are toddlers they tend to seek explanations in humanlike terms. This is called anthropomorphic thinking." At first the word *anthropomorphic* looks terribly unfamiliar. But if you study it you see that it begins to look something like *anthropology,* and you already know that this is the study of humankind. Connecting the new word to a more familiar word makes the new word easier to remember. In this example the new stimulus had a natural connection to an old stimulus. Often this is not the case, and you may *invent* a similarity. This is one key to *mnemonic devices,* or memory strategies, which are discussed in some detail in Chapter 14.

If you understand, and take advantage of, the laws of association, it will make it easier to acquire and retain information.

USING THE CONDITIONING PROCESS

Conditioning is a kind of learning that is somewhat mechanical in nature and does not require a high level of conscious awareness. Dogs, rats, and pigeons all can be conditioned. And, if you aren't insulted by the comparison, so can you. Indeed, you can't avoid being conditioned. It is only a question of whether or not your conditioning is going to serve you well or work against you. Conditioning is, in essence, the acquisition of habits.

There are two basic kinds of conditioning. *Classical conditioning* is the type that was studied by the great Russian physiologist Ivan Pavlov; it involves the learning of involuntary responses. *Operant conditioning* is the type that was studied by the American behaviorist B. F. Skinner; it involves, mainly, the learning of actions that have an effect on the external world.

Classical Conditioning

Pavlov discovered that a dog can be taught to salivate when it hears a tone of a specific pitch and frequency. (For convenience, this is often called a "bell," but this isn't really accurate.) Dogs aren't born salivating to tones. They learn the connection by being presented with the tone slightly before being fed. Food elicits salivation. Eventually, if the tone is associated with the food a number of times, the tone alone has the capacity to elicit salivation. Note that, once it has been conditioned, the dog seems to have no voluntary control over its behavior. It does not appear to us that it could will itself *not* to salivate when it hears the tone.

There are many human applications of the basic principle involved in classical conditioning. For example, let us say that before he studies Richard T. always pops a lemon drop in his mouth. One day he is out of lemon drops, tries to study, and has difficulty concentrating. The lemon drop, like the "bell" for the dog, triggers the study habit. Under these conditions the lemon drop is said to be a *conditioned stimulus*. And the studying response is a *conditioned response*. Almost any sight or sound, or even the time of day, can become a conditioned stimulus. They are the "triggers" that set off your involuntary habits.

In view of the fact that conditioned stimuli can't be avoided, and you *will* inevitably be conditioned, it is a good idea to consciously pick out sights, sounds, and times that are within your control. For example, it is all right to study with the radio on if it acts as a conditioned stimulus for you and you generally have no trouble finding a radio when you want to study. On the other hand, if you have conditioned yourself to study only when you are in the quiet section of the library, you may be in trouble. The library may be closed on a day or at a time when you need to prepare for an important test. Or it may simply be difficult to get to the library on certain occasions. You have, through conditioning, made yourself overly dependent on one particular conditioned stimulus—a quiet library.

If you are a parent, it is a good idea to condition yourself to study at the kitchen table with the television set on and the children making noise. Then you can study in snatches of time whenever you need to. This can backfire, of course. Elena L., a mother of two children, arranged for her husband to take the children to see a Disney movie on a Saturday afternoon. She settled down to study and found it difficult to work. It was too quiet!

In brief, use the classical conditioning process to your advantage by arranging that the cues, or conditioned stimuli, for your study behavior be familiar, convenient ones.

Operant Conditioning

B. F. Skinner's ground-breaking research on operant conditioning took place in the 1930s. The basic image of operant conditioning is of a rat pressing a lever to obtain a pellet of food. The rat learns to press the lever at a high rate if food is forthcoming. The food is said to be a *reinforcer,* a pay-off that has an effect on the conditioning process. And the rat's learning is *extinguished,* or unlearned, if the device is turned off and pressing the lever is made to be a waste of time. The kind of learning involved is called *operant* because the rat, so to speak, "operates" on its environment by pressing the lever.

Human examples of operant conditioning are plentiful. You turn the ignition switch in your car and are reinforced when the motor starts. If the battery is dead one morning, you try the switch a few times and then the switch-turning behavior is extinguished. Instead, you call a towing service or a friend. As another example, you are trying to train a child to make his or her bed in the morning on a regular basis. You can reinforce the desirable behavior with smiles, hugs, and praise—the tokens of love. Applications of operant conditioning principles to human beings go under the general heading of *behavior modification.*

The key to grasping the importance of operant conditioning in human affairs is to remember that *behavior is shaped by its own consequences.* Whatever you do produces an effect on the external world. This includes the social world, the world of other people. If your behavior has a positive consequence, it will be reinforced and tend to be repeated. If it has a negative consequence, or falls flat, it will tend to be extinguished.

Here are some highly specific applications of operant conditioning to student behavior:

1. Study in small, well-defined units of behavior (e.g., five pages). Stop when you have completed the unit and give yourself a small, easily obtained reinforcer such as a cup of coffee, time out with a child, or the opportunity to engage in any pleasant behavior. Note that what is and is not reinforcing is peculiar to the individual. Make a list of positive reinforcers that are easily available to you.

2. Many textbooks these days are published with a *study guide*, a softcover workbook with chapter outlines, learning objectives, lists of key terms, and practice tests. A key feature of study guides is a programmed review for each chapter. A *programmed review* breaks a subject into modest-sized chunks of readily grasped information. From time to time you are asked to fill in a blank, and then you check your work. Programmed reviews are an outgrowth of the teaching machine, a device invented by B. F. Skinner. Looked at in terms of operant conditioning, filling in a blank is the operant response. You are reinforced frequently by checking your work, and obtaining a series of small successes, as you go along.

3. In connection with item 2, your college may provide in the Learning Center *computer-assisted instruction*, presentations of programmed reviews of various subjects. This is becoming more and more common, is also an outgrowth of Skinner's work, and allows you to interact with the subject matter and obtain frequent reinforcement.

4. When you obtain a desirable grade on a test, share the score with a person who is likely to give you positive reinforcement in the form of praise or a kind word. This is, of course, a natural tendency. We look for recognition. However, it is important to *seek* a social support system actively. You need to know people who will reinforce your efforts. If you have a spouse, and he or she doesn't reinforce your academic successes, look for individuals who will.

THE ADVANTAGES OF INSIGHT LEARNING

Insight learning goes beyond conditioning, and it is the basic kind of learning involved when you acquire an understanding of concepts. The pioneer researcher on insight learning was Wolfgang Köhler, a Gestalt psychologist. (As mentioned in Chapter 5, the German word *Gestalt* means pattern, or organized whole. Gestalt psychologists studied perception, thinking, and learning as organized mental processes.)

One of Köhler's important experiments involved an ape called Sultan. Sultan learned, by his own efforts, that he could assemble two short sticks into one long stick that he could then use to rake in an orange that was outside his cage. At first Sultan was unable to solve the problem of how to obtain the orange. And then after a few days he suddenly put the sticks together, and he never forgot how to do it. Köhler says that Sultan reorganized his perceptual world in such a way that what were originally two independent parts became one unified whole (i.e., a Gestalt); likewise, an *insight* exists when a mind can bring together formerly disconnected parts into an organized, meaningful whole.

Here are three important points about insight learning: First, the acquisition of an insight is often initially frustrating. There may be a "dry" period when nothing seems to be happening. Second, the acquisition of an insight is always sudden, with a flash of abrupt understanding. Third, insights endure. We don't forget them.

The lack of even one key insight can cause great problems in learning. I remember when I was in the 10th grade at John Marshall High School in Los Angeles, the Latin teacher told us that we were going to conjugate verbs. I didn't have the slightest idea what *conjugate* meant. During the sixth week of instruction I received a failing notice. Then on the seventh week of instruction I suddenly said to myself: "Oh, I get it. Conjugate means something like *I run, you run, we run* and *ran* and *will run*. It has something to do with the present, the past, and the future." Believe it or not, this insight made all the difference. I began to do passing work. I earned a C in the course and took a second semester of Latin.

Herman K., age 29, father of five children and a life-insurance salesman, was taking a college mathematics class. The instructor gave a lecture involving circles. The formula for computing the circumference was given:

$$\text{Circumference} = \text{pi} \times \text{Diameter}$$

Herman could compute the circumference of various circles, but the formula was meaningless to him. He looked up *pi* in the dictionary. He discovered that it is the sixteenth letter of the Greek alphabet and that it is approximately 3.14159. This didn't help much. Then, while working on math problems, he had an insight; he thought: "Oh, I get it! All that pi means is that circular things ranging from tin cans to tires are roughly three times bigger around than they are across." This basic understanding, in his own terms, seemed to shed a bright light on the whole subject of circles in mathematics.

Karen O., age 33, was taking a psychology class. The teacher kept talking about *cognitive development* without defining the word *cognitive*. For a while Karen tried in vain to think of something familiar. Then suddenly something came to mind. It was the word *recognition*, and she had the insight that this familiar word and the new word cognitive were related. Karen thought, "To *recognize* is to *know again*. So *cognitive* all by itself must mean *knowing*. *Cognitive* obviously has something to do with knowing and conscious thought." She proceeded to follow the lecture with no difficulty.

Actively look for insights in anything you are learning. They will result in both deep comprehension and long-term retention of key concepts.

LEARNING TO LEARN

Approximately 40 years ago, Harry Harlow, a former president of the American Psychological Association, was studying the ability of rhesus monkeys to solve simple problems. He discovered that the monkeys got better and better at solving clusters of similar problems. A human example is provided by the individual who works a crossword puzzle every day. Little by little he or she becomes an expert at solving such puzzles and tends to work rapidly and easily.

Harlow labeled this principle *learning to learn*. It is more than just specific learning. It is a higher form of learning, a learning "above" the specific content of whatever is being studied. Whenever you learn, you also learn, subconsciously, certain nonspecific aspects of the material. These nonspecific aspects are difficult to specify in detail because they have an abstract quality. They include viewpoints, assumptions, familiarity with concepts, and improvement in vocabulary. These aspects are automatically transferred to new content to be learned, making your learning tasks easier as you progress up the academic ladder.

During my first two years of college I had a C+ average. In my last two years of college I had a B average. In my first year of graduate school I had a B+ average. By the time I was taking my last courses for a doctorate in psychology I had an A average. It just got easier and easier. It really did! I was learning to learn. The phenomenon is common, and doesn't apply just to me or a few people.

I include this information on learning to learn because I know that the common attitude of beginning college students is that college courses logically get harder and harder to learn because they become increasingly complex. It is, of course, true that the material itself becomes increasingly complex. However, this is usually more than offset by the learning to learn phenomenon.

So relax. You're not digging a deeper and deeper hole for yourself as you progress in college. Quite the contrary. Think of your progress upward as flying in a hot-air balloon that keeps dropping off restraining weight bags.

THE POSITIVE SIDE OF SLOW LEARNING

It is very common for a student to get discouraged because a part of his or her self-concept is, "I am a slow learner." In fact, however, very few college students are slow learners in *all* subjects. They will usually be fast learners in some subjects and slow learners in others. You will have a knack for, and a natural interest in, some subjects. I assure you that in these subjects you will probably be a fast learner. You will have no knack for, and no natural interest in, other subjects. It is almost certain that in these subjects you will be a slow learner.

Let us say that you are taking a required subject, and you are a slow learner in that subject. What should you do? The answer is straightforward. Apply the learning principles already set forth in this chapter and the study skills detailed in Chapter 5. Stick with the subject, persist, don't give up, use repetition—and you will learn the subject. Is it worth it? Of course it is, if passing the subject is important in terms of your long-term goals.

When I took introductory statistics at UCLA in my third year of college, I could barely move a decimal point. I didn't realize that when you multiply a *minus* times a *minus* it equals a *plus*. Statistical concepts didn't come easily to me. I was overwhelmed by a concept known as the *standard deviation*, a measure of the dispersion of scores in a population or a sample. But I stayed with the subject, often having to read the same page five, six, or seven times before key insights emerged. But I passed the course with a C, and I was proud of that C.

Now here's an odd thing. I have forgotten a lot of terms and concepts I learned in other courses in college, but I never forgot the statistical concepts. I eventually took graduate courses in statistics, and I have taught introductory statistics. In spite of some modest successes with statistics, I have no natural flair for the subject. Another odd thing is that I think I make a passable statistics teacher. I can anticipate the student's problems, and I am sympathetic because I suffered with the subject myself.

There is research in learning theory suggesting that slow learning often results in better long-term retention of subject matter. I compare the process to driving a first nail into a block of soft wood and a second nail into a block of hard wood. The first nail goes in easily; the second nail requires much pounding (i.e., repetition). If you wish to pry out the nails later, the first nail comes out easily. The second one is pried out with great effort. And that is the positive side of slow learning. Information that is acquired with effort and by a slow process is generally retained for a long time. It becomes a part of your long-term memory.

CONCLUDING REMARKS

We have all heard the saying, "You can't teach an old dog new tricks." This suggests that the adult student is "over the hill" and will be an incompetent learner, but actually the adult student is usually a very competent learner because he or she has a wealth of background and associations to draw on. The adult student also enjoys the fruits of the process known as *learning to learn*, discussed in this chapter.

In contrast to the saying about the "old dog," approximately twenty-five hundred years ago the Greek playwright Aeschylus said, "It is always in season for older persons to learn." Listen to what Aeschylus has to say and adopt the viewpoint that *you* will be a competent, effective adult student. The odds are that you are far from over the hill. It is more likely that you are in the prime of life in terms of your learning competence.

KEY POINTS TO REMEMBER

- Learning is an all-encompassing phenomenon. We learn all the time in all kinds of situations.
- A serviceable definition of *learning* is: A more or less permanent change in behavior, or a behavioral tendency, as a result of experience.
- The principal laws of association are (1) contiguity, (2) repetition, (3) attention, (4) pleasure-pain, and (5) similarity.
- *Classical conditioning* involves the learning of involuntary responses.
- Use the classical-conditioning process to your advantage by arranging that the cues, or conditioned stimuli, for your study behavior be familiar, convenient ones.
- *Operant conditioning* primarily involves the learning of actions that have an effect on the external world.
- Use the operant-conditioning process to your advantage by recognizing that behavior is shaped by its own consequences. In practical terms this means that you want to arrange positive reinforcers for your self-defined learning tasks.
- An *insight* exists when a mind can bring together formerly disconnected parts into an organized, meaningful whole.
- The process of *insight learning* implies that you should actively look for insights when you are learning concepts.
- The principle known as *learning to learn* indicates that whenever you learn you also learn, subconsciously, certain nonspecific aspects of the material.
- Slow learning often results in better long-term retention of information than does fast learning.

7

MOTIVATING YOURSELF

Of Incentives and Rewards

Anna N., age 29, works part time as a clerk at the cosmetics counter of a department store. She is married and is the mother of seven-year-old Shane. Anna recently applied for admission to a college, was accepted, and enrolled for three courses. She dropped out of one of them and completed the other two with a B and a C. She is disappointed in her academic performance. Her husband, Stanton, is not the problem, as he supports her educational aspirations. And Anna is a capable student when she puts forth a determined effort, so ability is not the problem. As Anna herself puts it, "I just don't seem to have any wind in my sails."

Steve V., age 34, is a short-order cook in a family restaurant and is the father of three children. He is divorced and has had a series of unstable relationships with several women. He pays regular child support to his ex-wife. Presently he lives alone in a threadbare apartment. If he takes a college course and decides to earn either an A or a B, he earns it. Over the past four years, however, he has enrolled for a total of 15 courses and has completed only 7 of them. He has great learning capacity, and he knows it. He is hard on himself. He says, "I know my own abilities. I should really amount to something in life—have a really good profession. I could give

67

my kids a better standard of living. I'm letting them down. I'm letting myself down."

What is wrong with Anna and Steve? The first answer that the mind suggests is, "they lack motivation." This answer is, in a sense, one explanation for their poor academic performance, but the answer doesn't go deep enough. Two more questions need to be asked and answered: (1) Why do they lack motivation? (2) What can they do about it?

Multiply Anna's and Steve's cases many times and you will find that lack of motivation is a general problem for many students in all colleges at all levels. It is extremely common for a student to have the ability to learn without the necessary motivation to go with it.

Here is a psychological formula of some value:

$$\text{Learning Ability} \times \text{Motivation} = \text{Academic Success}$$

The multiplication sign in this formula is used to symbolize the concept of an *interaction*. Two factors have an interactive, or multiplicative, relationship when they affect each other in a complex way. For example, learning ability affects motivation. Successful learning tends to have a positive effect on motivational level. Success begets success. However, it is also true that motivation supplies the initial "push" that makes effective learning possible. Thus, a low motivational level has an adverse impact on the learning process. Conversely, the presence of a high motivational level has a positive impact on the learning process.

If you identify to some extent with Anna and Steve, this chapter will help you understand your own motivational problems and how you can cope with them.

THE UNDERACHIEVEMENT SYNDROME

The term *underachiever* is often applied to a student who is working significantly below his or her learning ability. The problem with the word is that it tends to label the person and put him or her in a category. It is not much different from calling a person "a loser." The trouble with nouns such as *underachiever* and *loser* is that they summarize in a short-hand way the effects of a problem, or a set of problems, but they provide neither an analysis nor a solution.

Consequently, I avoid calling anyone an underachiever, even in my own mind. I prefer to speak of an *underachievement syndrome*. A *syndrome*, as it is often used in medicine and psychology, suggests a cluster of signs and symptoms suggesting the presence of pathology. This is a very helpful approach because it allows us to pinpoint trouble areas and look for corrective behaviors.

A *sign* is somewhat different from a symptom. A sign is experienced by others. In medicine, for example, a monitor reading of 160 over 110 is a clear sign of high blood pressure, even if there are no symptoms. If the patient comes into the office complaining of dizziness, weakness, or a hot feeling, these might be symptoms of high blood pressure.

Similarly, in the case of the underachievement syndrome, others might see signs of your lack of motivation that you yourself seem to be blind to. This is often because of an ego defense mechanism known as *denial of reality*, a psychological process that allows the individual to discount unpleasant facts. Denial of reality allows a person to live in what is known as a "Fool's Paradise." If the individual experiences, and is clearly aware of, certain aspects of an underachievement syndrome, then these would be symptoms.

The formal distinction between signs and symptoms blurs to some extent in real situations. Therefore, the distinction will not be overworked in the material that follows.

The aim of this section is to present a list of the key signs and symptoms of the underachievement syndrome. Looking over the list may be likened to looking in a mirror. You should not see something that is not there, but if the signs and symptoms apply to you, you are likely to recognize them. This list provides the first step in the correction of an underachievement syndrome. The list breaks down The Problem, an unmanageable giant, into a relatively manageable set of individual problems.

Here are some specific signs and symptoms of the underachievement syndrome:

1. *A tendency to procrastinate.* The student tends to say, "I'll study tomorrow," or "I'll study after the party," or "I'll wait until the weekend to write the term paper." You will notice that a key feature of procrastination is to put pleasure before an educational task.

2. *Aiming for only mediocre grades.* The student thinks, "I'm satisfied with a C. I'm getting by." Or worse yet, the student thinks, "In this course a D is good enough. It's not in my major, the D counts toward graduation, and I can average it out with a B in another course."

3. *Absence of anxiety before an examination.* Although excessive anxiety disrupts examination performance, moderate anxiety facilitates it. The student who has no anxiety before an examination is overly indifferent, and this has an adverse effect on test performance.

4. *Excessive socializing.* We all need friends and some sort of social life, but some students use socializing as a way of taking flight from the challenge of their textbooks.

5. *Boredom when the instructor is lecturing.* The student doesn't take notes but instead daydreams or doodles.

6. *Lack of participation during class discussions.* The student doesn't ask questions or make comments.

7. *Poor attendance.* When the instructor questions the student about a poor attendance record, various superficially plausible excuses are usually brought forth.

8. *Neglect of assignments.* Homework is not turned in, and deadlines on term papers are missed.

9. *Making an unrealistic class schedule.* The student signs up for too many classes, classes at inconvenient hours, or subjects that are too difficult. At first glance this may not seem to be a sign of underachievement, but it is. I will comment on this in the next section.

10. A *superficial overconfidence.* The student manifests a smug, I-know-it-all attitude.

It should be noted that the signs and symptoms overlap to some extent. This is reasonable in view of the fact that they are all manifestations of the general trait of underachievement.

CAUSES OF UNDERACHIEVEMENT

The underachievement syndrome can be explained. It is not good enough to say, "Natalie is lazy," or "Sawyer has no get-up-and-go." These are descriptions, not explanations.

In general, as was indicated earlier, it can be said that the underachievement syndrome is generated by a low level of motivation. However, this is a weak explanation at best. A low level of motivation is due to specific causes, which are identified below. More than one cause may be operating at one time in the case of a given individual.

Lack of Self-Confidence as a Student

The individual may be capable but may not see himself or herself as capable. Although the person may have high self-esteem in general, there is an absence of adequate self-esteem in the academic arena. There is an inner resistance to making a "big push" and to making a commitment to college work.

A Strong Fear of Failure

Related to lack of self-confidence, research has indicated that students with a strong fear of failure often take on an overly demanding, unrealistic class schedule. This may seem brave and confident, but it is often a form of false bravado. A heavy load usually results in poor grades and dropped classes. However, the poor performance now can be easily rationalized. I wrote about this in an earlier chapter. Students with a high need to avoid failure often "bite off more than they can chew."

Lack of a Well-Defined Identity

Some years ago the psychoanalyst Erik Erikson introduced into the theory of psychosocial development the related concepts of identity and identity crisis. A person has an *identity* when he or she has a robust sense of self, can say, "I know who I am," and feels comfortable in one or several significant social roles such as wife, husband, parent, teacher, healer, mechanic, business person, and so forth. An *identity crisis* exists when the person is confused or in a state of emotional conflict concerning the acceptance of a basic social role. Although in theory the crisis should be over toward the end of adolescence, the sad fact is that today more and more people are extending the crisis stage of psychosocial development well past adolescence. A lack of identity is associated with muddled dreams and goals and a general lack of direction in life.

A Troubled Relationship

Many students are either married, living together, or otherwise emotionally involved in a personal relationship. Sometimes there is fighting, misunderstandings, hurt feelings, and a lack of emotional closeness. Difficulties encountered with someone you love, or think you love, chip away at your peace of mind and work against your motivation as a student.

Lack of Intellectual Curiosity

Some students just don't have much interest in subjects that have no immediate impact on their lives. The unspoken thought in many general education courses, the courses that are required for graduation, is, "So what? Who cares?" I remember one student saying to me, "Who cares about history? It's just about a lot of dead people, and it all happened a long time ago." Another student enrolled in an astronomy course said, "I'm not interested in the planets and the stars. I'll never go there. They have nothing to do with my life. As far as I'm concerned everything I'm learning in this class is pointless." It is, of course, one of the instructor's responsibilities to point out the relevance and potential benefits of a subject. Unfortunately, quite a few students approach general education courses with a negative attitude.

Alcohol and Drug Abuse

Some students abuse alcohol and other drugs. Drugs, whether they may be stimulants or narcotics, have the general effect of blurring reality contact. Consequently, the kind of clear thinking that is required to look at life in an objective way and to be excited about the future is undermined. It is difficult for a person who abuses drugs to focus on the importance of education.

Lack of Well-Defined Long-Term Goals

Some students do not have dreams, or they feel that their dreams are unrealistic and unattainable. Consequently, they tend to avoid declaring a major field of study. They are unable to work in a persistent way toward a vocation.

No Family Role Models

Some students come from families that are not college oriented. Their parents did not go to college, and their brothers and sisters did not go to college. Such students often feel out of their element. There may be the unspoken, or even spoken, criticism from family members: "Who do you think you are? Do you think you're better than us?" The student wants to be loved and belong to the family, and the hostile attitude expressed by the family interferes with motivation.

Poor Nutrition

It may seem odd to include poor nutrition as a cause of a low motivational level. However, it is not at all uncommon for students to eat on the run, to depend too much on junk foods, to consume foods with hidden sugar (e.g., candy bars, soft drinks, and ice cream), to eat very few green vegetables, and so forth. The result is often a low level of B-complex vitamins, vitamins required in the synthesis of key neurotransmitters in the brain. Sugar abuse sometimes contributes to low blood sugar known as *hypoglycemia*, due to a physiological boomerang effect. Apathy and chronic fatigue are related to poor nutrition.

UNCONSCIOUS MOTIVES

Sigmund Freud, the father of psychoanalysis, said that the human mind is like an iceberg in that most of it exists below the surface. The conscious level of the mind is like the tip of the iceberg; the threshold of consciousness is like the water level; and the unconscious level of the mind is like the large, hidden base of the iceberg.

In freudian theory, the content of the unconscious level is said to be deposited there forcefully by an ego defense mechanism called repression. *Repression* is an automatic process by which the ego, the conscious self, rejects ideas and information that threaten self-esteem. Included in the repressed content are unconscious motives. Freud referred to these unconscious motives as "forbidden wishes," or desires that are prohibited by one's culture and family training. The two kinds of desires that are most likely to be repressed are aggressive and sexual ones. This is reasonable in view of the fact that the socialization of the individual requires the regulation of these particular desires.

Three examples follow that illustrate how unconscious motives can depress motivational level as a student.

Andrew E., 27, is married and the father of one child. He works 40 hours a week as a shoe clerk in a department store. He is majoring in marketing, is enrolled in three courses, and wants to rise to a managerial level at the store. Andrew has a substantial amount of repressed hostility toward his father, some of which is certainly justified as Andrew's father was controlling and dominating during Andrew's childhood. The reason the hostility is repressed is because Andrew is a traditional person with highly conventional attitudes, and he feels guilty about any conscious recognition of his hostility. One way that Andrew lets some of his hostility escape is by putting up a wall of resistance when an instructor lectures, particularly a self-confident, authoritative male instructor. Andrew just won't "take it" from an authority figure, a kind of substitute parent. He doesn't want to be told anything because he was told too much as a child. Consequently, he finds it difficult to attend to the content of a lecture, and he manifests a lack of interest in many of his college courses.

Deborah G., 33, is divorced and the mother of three children. Her goal is to become a registered nurse. She has completed 50 units in a pre-nursing program at a community college, and she will be able to transfer to a nursing school when she completes 20 more units. Her grades are not quite adequate. The nursing school requires a B average, and she falls a little below that average at present. It is her hope that she can improve her grade point average when she takes the additional 20 required units. Her developmental history as a child and adolescent involved a pattern of verbal abuse from her parents, during which she was made to feel stupid, ugly, and inadequate. Her natural hostility toward them has been distorted and converted into hostility toward herself. Unconsciously, she doesn't feel she deserves the best in life. She displays a *self-defeating pattern*, a pattern in which she consistently sets herself up for her own failures. Consequently, she is not motivated to excel in her courses.

Ramona M., 26, is single and lives alone in an inexpensive apartment, works part-time at a fast-food restaurant, and reads two romance novels a week. She is majoring in English literature and would like a career that combines teaching English with creative writing. She is an introverted, quiet woman with only a few close friends. Her developmental history was one of emotional rejection. She felt that she could obtain the tokens of love from her parents only by being a very, very good child. And even when there was approval she felt she had worked too hard for it. Unconsciously, she is looking for the perfect lover to give her all of the unconditional affection she missed as a child. From an educational viewpoint the unfortunate consequence of this is that she tends to develop crushes on her male instructors. She is very discreet and keeps her feelings to herself. Freud called this phenomenon the *positive transference*, the unconscious transference of a child's wish for the ideal parent onto a parental substitute. The positive transference is the "honeymoon" stage of a relationship. During this stage all is well and Ramona works hard to please her instructor because she yearns for his love. Unfortunately, as he becomes a real, demanding person with an individual personality that doesn't fit her ideal fantasy, she moves into a second stage called the *negative transference*. Now he is perceived as incompetent, uninteresting, superficial, and not worth listening to. At this point Ramona begins to perform poorly in the class and earns a final grade well below her academic ability.

COPING WITH YOURSELF

If you display some of the signs and symptoms of the underachievement syndrome, you need to cope with yourself. You can target specific causes that apply to you and gain insight into your own unconscious motives. By the application of will and intelligence, you can discover effective ways to overcome personal blocks to your positive, forward-looking tendencies in life. You may find value in the following list of coping strategies.

- Avoid labeling yourself as an underachiever. Instead, say that you display some of the signs and symptoms of underachievement. The first approach tends to freeze you in time and makes underachievement a permanent trait of your personality. The second approach is hopeful and includes the assumption that you can change your behavior.
- Face reality. If the signs of underachievement seem to be present, then fully acknowledge them. You can't cope with something that you say doesn't exist. Otherwise, you will be shadow boxing with ghosts.
- In your first semester or two of college enroll in classes that do not appear too difficult. Also, take only two or three classes, not a full load of five or six. The aim of these actions is to assure some early successes in order to bolster your self-confidence as a student. This will also undermine a general fear of failure.
- Work on defining your identity. Ask yourself who you really are and where you want to be in life five and ten years from now. Explore in your imagination the various social roles that seem both acceptable and possible to you. Try to select one road in life. It is impossible to travel down two or more roads. You have only one life to live.
- Do your best to make a relationship or a marriage work. Try to be an understanding person. Make an effort to see the other person's point of view. Learn effective ways to communicate without being either too passive or too aggressive. Strive for ways to replace emotional distance with emotional closeness. It is difficult to be a motivated student in a hostile atmosphere marred by bickering and misunderstanding.
- If you abuse drugs, give this problem a high priority. It is essential to find ways to manage this aspect of your life if you want to become an effective student.
- Explore your personal dreams. Think about your long-term goals. (This is related to finding an identity.) If you find that you have few if any positive images for yourself in the future, try to develop them.

- If your family presents no role models for academic achievement, borrow models from friends, acquaintances, and your reading. David G.'s parents owned a liquor store and were high school graduates. David himself, now a practicing clinical psychologist, admired the books of Sigmund Freud when he was an adolescent and today he keeps a bust of Freud on his desk. It is obvious that he admires Freud, identifies with him, and uses him as a role model, rather than his parents.

- Be sure your nutrition is adequate, or even better than adequate. Avoid foods high in refined sugar and/or saturated fats. Obtain plenty of complex carbohydrates, fruits, and vegetables with natural fiber. You also need ample protein. Milk, eggs, cheese, meat, and fish are traditional high-protein foods with all the essential amino acids. Cut down on saturated fat by selecting non-fat or low-fat milk and cheese, restricting egg yolks, skinning chicken, and broiling meat. Consider the possibility of taking a daily multiple-vitamin capsule as a nutritional supplement.

- Make an attempt to gain some insight into unconscious motives. If you let them run your life, the situation is somewhat like that of the dog that was wagged by its tail. You are a conscious, thinking being, and you can use this consciousness to see into the darkest and deepest recesses of your personality. Ask yourself if unfinished business from your childhood and adolescence is generating a negative attitude toward your studies and your instructors. Decide that you have a free will and do not have to obey the dictates of your unconscious motives.

- Make your analysis in writing. Several of the coping strategies outlined above suggest that you engage in a process of exploration or analysis in order to enhance insight and understanding. This can be best accomplished with the aid of a writing instrument. If you actually put your thoughts down on paper, you give them concrete form and it is then possible to come to better grips with them. Sigmund Freud undertook a ten-year self-analysis, and it was in writing.

OF INCENTIVES AND REWARDS

The two master principles of self-motivation are:

1. Provide yourself with incentives.
2. Give yourself rewards.

My dictionary defines an incentive as that which incites to action; a motivating force. An *incentive* in motivational psychology is usually thought of as existing somewhere in the future. An incentive is *anticipated*. That is why I have laid so much stress on dreams and long-term goals in this chapter. Although residing in the future, they provide the stimulus for action in the present. Sometimes people are criticized for being dreamers and are maligned as people who "chase rainbows." It is, of course, possible to spin dreams and never act on them. On the other hand, all great human accomplishments are the result of dreaming first. Thomas Edison dreamed of developing an incandescent bulb that would burn for hours and hours, and today we enjoy electric lights. Sir Alexander Fleming dreamed of a drug that would help us fight bacterial infections, and today we have penicillin and other antibiotic agents. Five years ago one of my students dreamed of becoming a CPA and opening his own private practice. Today he is a successful accountant.

You need a personal dream for the future. Work on it, develop it, and make it come true.

The concept of a reward is closely related to the concept of an incentive. However, a reward is usually thought of as close in time and given immediately following an action. In the psychology of motivation and learning, a reward is usually objectively defined as a *reinforcer*, a stimulus that has the objective effect of increasing a category of responses (e.g., study habits). Consequently, you should reward, or reinforce, your behavior often. This has the effect of *maintaining* your motivation. I will write about this at greater length in Chapter 9 under the heading of *avoiding procrastination*, so let's save some of the details for that section.

CONCLUDING REMARKS

Whenever your motivation as a student tends to fall off and you wonder how you can go on, just remember that the arrow of life points toward the future. Your responsible behavior today will pay off tomorrow. Keep your mind on this basic principle. Don't let the temptations and distractions of the day detour you from your course. The immature mind is like a child playing in the park, chasing every ball and butterfly, whereas the mature mind is like an adult who is walking through the park to reach a destination. The adult enjoys the grass, the flowers, and the trees, but *stays on the path*. Try to keep this image in mind. And stay on your path.

KEY POINTS TO REMEMBER

- Here is a psychological formula that shows the relationship of learning to motivation:

    Learning Ability × Motivation = Academic Success

- The *underachievement syndrome* consists of a set of signs and symptoms, all of which point to a low level of motivation as a student.
- The chapter identifies 10 signs and symptoms of the underachievement syndrome. Three of them are: (1) A tendency to procrastinate, (2) boredom when the instructor is lecturing, and (3) a superficial overconfidence.
- The chapter identifies a cluster of causes of underachievement. Three of them are: (1) Lack of self-confidence as a student, (2) lack of a well-defined identity, and (3) lack of well-defined long-term goals.
- Unconscious motives, existing as forbidden wishes at the deeper levels of the personality, may depress motivational level as a student.
- The chapter presents a number of ways you can cope with the underachievement syndrome. Five of them are: (1) Avoid labeling yourself as an underachiever, (2) work on defining your identity, (3) explore your personal dreams, (4) borrow role models from friends, acquaintances, and your reading, if your family presents no such models for academic achievement, and (5) make an attempt to gain some insight into unconscious motives.
- The two master principles of self-motivation are: (1) Provide yourself with incentives and (2) give yourself rewards.
- Whenever your motivation as a student tends to fall off, and you wonder how you can go on, keep your mind on the fact that the arrow of life points toward the future.

8

COPING WITH MATH ANXIETY

Greek Letters Don't Terrify Greek Children

The poet Carl Sandburg once said, "Arithmetic is where the answer is right and everything is nice and you can look out of the window and see the blue sky—or the answer is wrong and you have to start all over and try again and see how it comes out this time." Carl Sandburg was a poet of the people if ever there was one, and in reading his words there automatically comes to mind a picture of a child struggling with sums or trying to understand the mysteries of subtraction.

Mathematics have not baffled only Carl Sandburg and children. If the subject is pursued to its farthest reaches, it is filled with unanswered questions. The philosopher Bertrand Russell, one of the leading mathematicians of the twentieth century, said: "Mathematics may be defined as the subject in which we never know what we are talking about, nor whether what we are saying is true."

If you have problems with mathematics, therefore, your first consolation should be that you are not alone. You have good company in Carl Sandburg, Bertrand Russell, and countless thousands of others.

It is important to find practical ways to cope with math anxiety for three basic reasons: (1) General education requirements usually specify one or two mathematics courses, (2) many academic majors require several mathematics courses, and (3) clear thinking in mathematics contributes to clear thinking in general.

AN ALL-TOO-COMMON PROBLEM

As the opening remarks of this chapter suggest, math anxiety is an all-too-common problem. I have conducted informal surveys of my own students, have talked to many college instructors about the problem, and have discussed math anxiety with numerous students in private discussions, and I do not think that it is any exaggeration at all to say that perhaps one-half of college students suffer from math anxiety ranging in intensity from moderate to severe. And in earlier chapters I have made no secret of the fact that I too have suffered from math anxiety.

Math anxiety can be defined as follows: a tendency to feel fear and/or vague feelings of apprehension when one is trying to learn a mathematical concept, attempting to work a mathematical problem, or taking an examination.

Here are some responses obtained in writing from students that suggest the kinds of experiences and thoughts associated with math anxiety:

Student 1 writes, "I've never been good at arithmetic. When I add or subtract, half of the time I make mistakes. I don't trust my answers, and I have to compulsively check and double-check my work over and over again. Consequently, I take 'forever' to complete a test. Even when a calculator is allowed, I have a problem and have to double-check everything because I keep wondering if I've made a mistake and have punched the wrong buttons."

Student 2 writes, "I have so much math anxiety that my heart starts to pound and my palms start to sweat when I'm just *thinking* of signing up for a basic algebra course."

Student 3 writes, "I think I'm allergic to Greek symbols. I'm taking a statistics course right now. There's a Greek symbol called sigma that's used a lot. It looks sort of like a capital M sideways. Every time I see it I'm thrown for a loop. I begin to shake a little. And that's not the only Greek symbol! The damn stat book is filled with them. Sometimes I want to throw the book in the trash can. I'll never understand why they have to use Greek symbols instead of ordinary letters."

Student 4 writes, "When I sit down to take an algebra test and see the problems and the symbols, I always tighten up. I begin to breathe rapidly, and it feels like there's a belt around my chest. I start to think that no matter what answer I come up with I can't be sure that it will be right. I feel like I'm walking in a fog."

Student 5 writes, "One of my problems with mathematics is that it seems to me to be a subject without a heart. It's as cold as ice. I'm taking a math course now and the teacher strikes me the same way as the subject— remote, cold, unemotional, and uncaring."

THE ROOTS OF MATH ANXIETY

There are several causes of math anxiety. Let's identify some of the more common ones. It has been said that every problem contains the seeds of its own destruction. By making an analysis of the causes of math anxiety, you will be in a position to employ the specific antianxiety strategies presented toward the latter part of the chapter. Keep in mind that more than one of the identified causes can be operating in a single individual.

A Long Time Ago

It is quite possible that five, six, seven, or more years have elapsed since you took your last math class. You think, "That was a long time ago. I've forgotten everything I ever learned. I'm rusty, and I don't know if I can just step in and start learning again." This is a basic cause of math anxiety— the conviction that too much time has passed, and there has been too much forgetting.

The Way Mathematical Concepts Are Presented

It is common for an adult student to say, "I had some bad math teachers when I was a kid. And they turned me off the subject." It can be argued that this is a rationalization. After all, other students in the classroom appeared to learn, earned high grades, grew up to become engineers, and so forth. However, the complaint often *does* in fact have some truth to it.

A body of research evidence in educational psychology on how children learn mathematical concepts suggests that they need *concrete examples,* examples that include the actual handling of measuring instruments, the counting of markers on a rod, and the ordering of objects by size and shape. This approach is taken in a few grammar schools, but not most. The method was first recommended by Maria Montessori, an Italian educator who did her major research more than 70 years ago. Max Wertheimer, father of Gestalt psychology, recommended a similar approach in his book *Productive Thinking,* published in 1959.

Because concepts are often presented on a blackboard without an opportunity on the child's part to translate the concept into a physical form, countless children only half grasp the fundamental ideas of mathematics. It is no wonder that they become progressively lost and confused as they go along.

The students who do well in mathematics classes in the early years are the ones who have a natural flair for the subject, and this is perhaps a relatively small percentage of children. The rest of the children often go begging. They are fortunate if they happen to have parents or older siblings who can help them out, or if tutoring can be obtained. But often this is not the case.

Right-Brain Dominance

The brain has two hemispheres, the left and the right. The nervous system structure that connects the two hemispheres, the *corpus callosum* (i.e., thick body), makes it possible for the two sides of the brain to communicate with each other. This structure is sometimes cut by a neurosurgeon in an effort to stop the suffering of persons who are prone to chronic epileptic seizures. In the 1960s Roger W. Sperry of the California Institute of Technology studied the intelligence, personality, and mental processes of persons with a cut corpus callosum.

Sperry's research suggests that the left hemisphere mediates such mental processes as verbal, logical, and mathematical thought. The right hemisphere mediates mental processes like spatial imagery and pattern perception. If someone asks you to define a spiral staircase, and you answer, "It's a series of ascending steps revolving around a common center," you have used words and are processing the answer on the left side of your brain. On the other hand, if you answer by making a corkscrew-like gesture with your hand and index finger and say, "Oh, you know, it looks like this sort of," you are processing the answer with the right side of your brain. If you give a good verbal definition and combine it with the gesture, you are coordinating the activity of both sides of your brain.

It is a popular idea that some people may be left-brain dominant and others may be right-brain dominant. This doesn't mean that one can't use the nondominant hemisphere. It just means that the automatic preference is for the dominant one, and the other one gets sort of "lazy." If you can carry a tune easily, like to paint or draw, enjoy dancing, frequently try your hand at creative writing, and find yourself irritated by people who always insist on being logical, it is possible that you are right-brain dominant. If so, it is to be expected that you would have no natural attraction to mathematics. And it is to be also expected that you would be a slow learner of mathematical concepts.

Overly Rapid Teaching

It is a common mistake for teachers at all levels to present mathematical concepts too rapidly. There are two principal reasons for this. First, the teacher probably has a natural flair for mathematics. He or she was a highly competent student, learned the concepts easily, and was attracted to the career of mathematician. Individuals such as these often end up teaching the subject. However, this sort of person has little natural empathy for the mental anguish of the person who grasps and retains mathematical concepts with difficulty. Consequently, there is a tendency to lecture too rapidly, to erase problems too quickly, and in general to be impatient with the student's learning problems.

A second reason is that the instructor has *overlearned* the subject. He or she has gone over the concepts so many times that they are "old stuff." This contributes to teaching rapidly and abridging explanations of difficult concepts.

To their credit, many teachers and instructors with the above tendencies are aware of them and try to check them. Others, however, do not.

Cognitive Development

Research originally conducted by Jean Piaget in Europe suggests that human beings go through four principal stages of cognitive development. *Cognitive development* refers to the growth of the conscious thought processes from birth to adulthood. The names of the four stages, and their associated ages, are as follows: (1) sensorimotor (birth–2 years), (2) preoperational (2–7), (3) concrete operations (7–12), and (4) formal operations (12–adulthood). Without going into detail about the key mental features of the four stages, it is important to note that mathematical concepts are first taught in grammar school during stage three, the stage of concrete operations. Notice that we meet the word *concrete* again. During stage three the child *can* grasp mathematical concepts but *only if* these concepts have the capacity to be represented in the real world by a concrete operation. A *concrete operation* is a tangible, physical one that can be demonstrated to the senses. Consequently, if the mathematical statement is made that $2 + 3 = 5$, a concrete demonstration of this concept consists of placing two pennies in one little group and three pennies in an adjacent group. Then the operation of "plus" is demonstrated by bringing the two little groups together into a larger group of five coins.

Concrete mathematical operations can become quite complex. Fractions are an example. Nonetheless, fractions *can* be demonstrated in terms of pieces of a pie. Therefore, fractions are essentially concrete and can be grasped by children in the stage of concrete operations.

Algebra, on the other hand, is *not* concrete. Let's say that an average 10-year-old is presented with the following problem: $x + 7 = 10$. What does x equal? Assume that the child is baffled. Now the adult explains that x has to be 3 because 3 plus 7 equals 10. The child seems to comprehend. Now the child is presented with a new problem: $x + 15 = 20$. What does x equal? The 10-year-old is likely to answer, "3." If you, the adult, say, "No, it's 5," the child is likely to become cross with you and say, "You just told me that x is 3!" This is because children in the stage of concrete operations cannot grasp that x is a variable and can be *any* number.

In order to grasp a concept such as, "There is a variable designated x," a child needs to be in Piaget's fourth stage of cognitive development, *formal operations*. Key attributes of formal operations include the ability to think in abstract terms and to reflect on one's own thinking (i.e., to think about thinking). A student is not receptive to concepts in algebra until he or she has entered the fourth stage, and this is usually around the age of 12, 13, or even a little older.

This is one of the ways my own mathematical education went wrong. I took introductory algebra in junior high school at the age of 11, and, looking back, I was able to think only in concrete terms. Therefore algebra meant little or nothing to me. Consequently, I earned a D and decided that I was no good at mathematics. It was a difficult and gradual process to rid myself of this idea.

The Language of Mathematics

Mathematics is communicated in a language all its own. Instead of ordinary English, we encounter numerals and special symbols. A first problem is that the language of a particular subject in mathematics such as algebra, statistics, or calculus is often unfamiliar to the beginning student.

A second problem is that the language of mathematics is nonredundant. *Nonredundant* means that mathematics is communicated in sets of symbols with neither overlaps nor room for error. This is, in one sense, an advantage because it allows for absolute precision in communication. For a novice, however, it presents formidable barriers because it allows no latitude for mistakes. If you make one mistake, the communication process breaks down.

For example, study the following sentence. "My motorcicle were sitting in the hot son." Two words are misspelled and there is an error of agreement in the verb. Nonetheless, it is easy to perceive what the correct sentence should be: "My motorcycle was sitting in the hot sun." This is because ordinary English is *redundant*, allowing plenty of margin for error.

On the other hand, study the following mathematical sentence: "The standard deviation of the sample = 24.8." If there *is* an error, you can't tell. Actually, the student misplaced the decimal, and the answer should have been 2.48. By making the "small" error of placing the decimal just one position to the right, *all* meaningful communication was lost. If, in a formula, a minus sign is incorrectly placed where a plus sign should be, the entire sense of the formula changes. In other words, mathematics, being a nonredundant language, makes no allowance for seemingly small, trivial errors.

Consequently, it is in the very nature of mathematics itself to be difficult for some students. Again, students who are attracted to "right-brain thinking," thinking in general patterns and big pictures, will find mathematics much too constricting and overly detailed because of the demands of mathematics' nonredundant language.

An Inferiority Complex

Finally, the kinds of causal factors I have cited in this section tend to converge and produce in a relatively high percentage of students what can be called a *mathematical inferiority complex*, a set of interrelated ideas that suggest to the individual that one is a hopelessly incompetent, ineffective learner when it involves the mathematical arena.

Alfred Adler, one of the early pioneers in psychotherapy, is the one who originally coined the term *inferiority complex*. He said that it arises when a person's will to power is frustrated. The *will to power*, according to Adler, is an inborn striving tendency; it dictates that we should try to become as competent and effective as we can be. Consequently, children and adolescents usually *do* strive to grasp mathematical concepts. When they fail more than once, they develop an inferiority complex.

This complex, the end state of an adverse learning history, plays a large role in math anxiety and the avoidance of courses in mathematics.

SPECIFIC ANTIANXIETY STRATEGIES

If you suffer from math anxiety, the specific antianxiety strategies described below may help you reduce it. It is clear that the reduction of anxiety will help you function more effectively as a student because excessive anxiety tends to disrupt both learning and test performance. However, keep in mind that *moderate* anxiety facilitates both learning and performance. So the goal is not to eliminate *all* anxiety but to reduce it to realistic proportions.

- Remember that the passage of time does not necessarily destroy learning. The fact that you took your last math class a long time ago is not as significant as you might think. True, you probably can't recall much right now as an act of will, but that is because the stimulus is missing. By listening to a lecture or studying a textbook, dormant memory traces will be activated. And you may be pleasantly surprised to discover how much comes back to you. This phenomenon, known as *savings*, is a basic one. And you can count on it to some extent.
- If you grasp mathematical concepts poorly or only half understand them because of the way that mathematical concepts were presented to you as a child or adolescent, make your reentry into the subject in shallow psychological water. Take courses with titles such as "Introduction to College Mathematics" or "Elementary Algebra" before you take more complex courses. Or, if you feel that you are very deficient, take one or two remedial courses. These are often offered by either the Learning Center or the Math Department itself. Although remedial courses may carry no credit toward a four-year degree, they are not a waste of time because they provide the foundation that makes later academic success possible.
- Let's say that you are, or think you are, right-brain dominant. Consequently, you are convinced that you grasp mathematical concepts with difficulty. This may be true, but this doesn't mean that you *can't* grasp mathematical concepts. It just means that your left brain is sort of "lazy" when it approaches these concepts. When a child has a

lazy eye, and the two eyes don't coordinate, an ophthalmologist often places an eyepatch on the dominant eye, forcing the lazy eye to go to work. You can do something similar when you approach a math course. Make your left brain go to work. Give the math course twice as much study time as any other course; imagine that it is two courses instead of one; spend plenty of time in working problems on scratch paper; use repetition—your lazy left brain will get the message. You will find that its ability to grasp mathematical concepts is not quite as poor as you thought it was.

- If you encounter an instructor who presents mathematical concepts too rapidly for you to grasp, don't make the disastrous mistake of concluding that he or she is a genius and that you are an idiot. The truth of the matter is that it is the instructor who should be ashamed. He or she is not doing the job well. Cope by getting as much as you can out of the classes. Use the classes to take rough notes. These notes will provide clues to what is important even if you don't understand the concepts at the time of presentation. Then spend plenty of time studying the concepts directly from the book on your own. See the teacher during office hours and ask questions about concepts that seem difficult to grasp.

- Keep in mind that one of the reasons why you may be having difficulty with mathematics as an adult is because you were exposed to abstract concepts when you were in the stage of cognitive development known as *concrete operations*. It is important to realize that you, as an adult, have the capacities associated with *formal operations*. You can think in abstract terms and comprehend material you could not comprehend when you were a child. Think of yourself as a different person from the child you once were. You are far from identical to that child, and you have capacities the child did not have.

- Remember that the nature of the language of mathematics presents problems of its own. It is nonredundant. Consequently, it has no margin for error. This is not the way ordinary English is. Consequently, you must make a conscious shift and decide that the learning of mathematical concepts, the writing of formulas, and the working of problems will require slow, precise work. This general approach also applies to studying a textbook. One page in a mathematics book can easily have as much conceptual content as five pages in a history textbook.

- Translate all symbols into ordinary English. Mathematics uses various brief symbols, including Greek ones. These symbols, taken together, constitute a kind of shorthand. This has its advantages because it allows for a lot of information to be communicated in a small space, but if you don't know exactly what a symbol means you are walking down a blind alley. You have to find a way to turn the lights on. The way is straightforward if you are able to express the meaning of the symbol in an ordinary English phrase or sentence. For example, the symbol x is commonly used in algebra. A translation is: "The symbol x stands for any number. It can be 2, 47, or anything."

Toward the beginning of the chapter a student was quoted who had an aversion to the capital Greek letter *sigma*. A translation of the symbol is: "Add up all the numbers." That is *all* that it means. Whenever *sigma* is seen, and this sentence comes to mind, all of the mystery and anxiety is gone and you will know what to do. When an obscure symbol seems to be inducing anxiety, just think to yourself, "Greek symbols don't terrify Greek children."

- Take advantage of the desensitization process. The *desensitization process* is a natural learning process in which repeated exposure to a fearful stimulus robs that stimulus of its power to evoke anxiety. The process is often used in *desensitization therapy*, a kind of behavioral therapy pioneered by the psychiatrist Joseph Wolpe. For example, a person with a snake phobia is presented with guided fantasies graded from mild to powerful involving encounters with snakes. Repeated involvement with the fantasies reduces the fear of snakes in the real world. (It is important that the fantasies have positive outcomes.) It is also possible to do *in vivo* desensitization instead of using fantasies. In this second method the stimuli can be pictures in books, trips to a zoo, and so forth. You can use both processes in overcoming math anxiety. Before a test, with your eyes closed, induce a daydream in which you see yourself taking the test and working effectively. Allow anxiety to rise, keep the daydream going, and eventually your anxiety will subside. Some desensitization has taken place. Repeat the daydream several times before a test, and you may find that when you are actually taking the test you will be much calmer than you might have been otherwise. *In vivo* desensitization is automatic and does not require special techniques such as daydreams. Just by taking a math course, studying the textbook, and so forth, you are automatically presenting yourself with the stimuli that bring about anxiety reduction. The important thing is to tolerate anxiety, stick with the course, and in the long run anxiety is likely to subside.

- Keep in mind that a mathematics inferiority complex is just that, a *complex*. A complex is a set of ideas, *not* a fact. Your complex may tell you that you are incompetent in mathematics, but this does not mean that you actually *are* incompetent. You have to examine the ideas in the complex and ask yourself, "Are these *really* true about me? Or are they just old ideas that carry over from bad experiences in the past?" It will help you to reduce anxiety by saying to yourself, "I may have a math inferiority complex, but it doesn't have me."

- Seek tutorial help. It is quite likely that the Learning Center at your college has a tutorial program. Working on a one-to-one basis with a tutor, or in small groups of three or four people, it is often possible to come to grips with mathematical concepts. The tutor is usually a student who works on a part-time basis, earned a high grade in a given subject, and has had recent experience with the obstacles and problems of a particular class. When you take an examination and *know that you know* the key concepts, anxiety is automatically reduced.

- Take a special course designed to reduce math anxiety. Such a course may be offered by the Counseling Center, the Learning Center, the Psychology Department, or sometimes the Math Department itself. The course offered at the college where I teach is called "Math Without Fear." Such courses often are brief, lasting approximately eight weeks, with one hour of instruction per week. They may not carry credit toward a four-year degree, but they are well worth the time spent in them if they have the effect of reducing your math anxiety.

KEY POINTS TO REMEMBER

- Math anxiety is a very common problem. Perhaps one-half of all college students suffer from it to some degree.

- *Math anxiety* can be defined as follows: A tendency to feel fear and/or vague feelings of apprehension when one is trying to learn a mathematical concept, attempting to work a mathematical problem, or taking an examination.

- The chapter presents a number of causes of math anxiety. Six of them are: (1) The conviction that too much time has elapsed since one's last math class along with the idea that one has forgotten everything, (2) the presentation of mathematical concepts in childhood without concrete examples, (3) right-brain dominance, perhaps associated with the lack of a natural flair for mathematics, (4) the presentation of abstract mathematical concepts when one was in the nonreceptive stage of cognitive development known as *concrete operations*, (5) the nonredundant nature of mathematical language, and (6) the formation of an inferiority complex.

- The chapter presents a number of specific antianxiety strategies. Seven of them are: (1) Remember that the passage of time does not necessarily destroy learning, (2) make your reentry into the subject of mathematics in shallow psychological water, (3) use practical methods to make a "lazy" left brain go to work, (4) cope with the nonredunant nature of mathematical language by making a conscious shift and deciding that the learning of mathematical concepts requires slow, precise work, (5) translate all symbols into ordinary English, (6) take advantage of the desensitization process, (7) keep in mind that a mathematics inferiority complex is just that, a *complex*, a set of ideas, rather than a fact.

- Remember these two sentences and recite them to yourself whenever you feel anxiety rising:

  "I may have a math inferiority complex, but it doesn't have me."
  "Greek symbols don't terrify Greek children."

9

ORGANIZING YOUR TIME

Are You Biting Off More Than You Can Chew?

Barbara D. is 31, divorced, the mother of three children, a life insurance agent, and a college student. She was in my office recently and I was advising her on her class schedule. She made the following comment: "Wouldn't it be nice to have a time machine? Then I could study all day Tuesday. Then I could go back to the same Tuesday morning and clean house, bake, make a great dinner, and spend quality time with the kids. Then I could go back again to Tuesday morning and sell life insurance all day. Then I could go back and. . . . " Her voice trailed off.

Then Barbara gave herself a little shake and said, "Well, I don't have a time machine. And never will have one. So I'd better face reality and learn to manage my time intelligently. I've got to get rid of this feeling that I'm always overwhelmed, that I can't do everything I've got to do no matter how hard I try."

Later in the interview Barbara said, "I've got to get organized." I have heard this phrase in various versions countless times from students.

It is extremely common for adults in college to feel somewhat like Barbara. There is the conviction that there is too much to do and not enough time to do it. Consequently, there is a constant time pressure on the individual. It is stressful and interferes with the quality of one's job, academic, and parental performance.

This chapter introduces the concept of time management. *Time management* is a voluntary process in which specific skills are used to reduce stress and increase effectiveness by learning to budget time in a rational manner. Implied in this definition is the idea that time is a commodity, a kind of psychological "money." This appears to be natural to human beings, and it is reflected in our ordinary speech. We talk of "spending time," "wasting time," and "saving time." So we perceive time much as we perceive money. Like money, it has value. Like money, it can be saved or wasted. Like a weekly paycheck, there are only so many hours to spend in a given week. Almost everyone is familiar with the concept of budgeting money. A less familiar concept is the budgeting of time, but it is just as important.

The principal aim of this chapter is to offer practical suggestions that will help you budget and manage time effectively.

THE TIME-PRESSURE SYNDROME

The *time-pressure syndrome*, a common one in our fast-paced, modern world, consists of a set of negative and self-defeating attitudes and behaviors. Time itself becomes a source of stress and is perceived as a kind of enemy that opposes one's success. Some of the signs and symptoms of the time-pressure syndrome are as follows:

1. *Always in a hurry.* Everything is done at a too-rapid pace. A spouse or children are called "slow-pokes" because they don't dress or do other things fast enough. There just doesn't seem to be enough hours in the day to take classes, study, do assignments, work, and take care of children. Another name for the time-pressure syndrome is the "hurry-up sickness."

2. *A constant sense of urgency.* Too many things seem to demand immediate attention, and the individual lives in a perpetual crisis atmosphere. There are deadlines to meet. The student thinks, "The book report is due tomorrow. And I haven't written a line!" Or, "There

is a test coming up in two days and I don't know when I can sit down and study for it!" Daily responsibilities, such as shopping for a child's birthday present, take on the same urgent quality.

3. *Impatience.* The individual seems to be impatient with everything and everybody. When other people are talking, one wishes they would get to the end of their remarks more quickly. Sometimes the individual interrupts and finishes sentences for other people. Although this is grossly impolite, there is the rationalization, "Oh, I knew what they were going to say anyway." This trait of impatience carries over into the classroom. It is a truism that many instructors and college professors enjoy pontificating and holding forth on a subject at length. The impatient student often finds this irritating and close to unendurable.

4. *Hostility.* Time pressure generates frustration, and frustration induces aggression. Consequently, the individual finds himself or herself in a chronic state of low-grade hostility. Behaviors suggestive of this state are snapping at loved ones, putting others down with mean little remarks, failing to laugh at jokes told by others, and talking negatively about instructors behind their backs. Sometimes this kind of hostility is called *free-floating* because it is just *there*, like a cloud of poison gas, and it attaches itself to anything in its way.

5. *Doing two things at once.* The individual writes checks for monthly bills while talking to a friend on the phone. Or the individual has a textbook open on the sink while trying to cook dinner for the family. Two activities must be crammed into the slot allotted for one because there is the nagging thought, "There just isn't enough time to do everything I have to do."

You may recognize from these signs and symptoms a pattern that has been called *Type A behavior.* The terms *time-pressure syndrome* and *Type A behavior* have approximately the same meaning. About twenty years ago the cardiologists Meyer Friedman and Ray H. Rosenman identified Type A behavior as a risk factor in heart disease. Its role in heart disease has been subject to assessment and evaluation, and it is not the aim of this section to associate it with a health condition, but the existence of the pattern itself seems real enough. And it seems self-evident that the pattern is a disruptive one that interferes with one's long-term effectiveness as a student. That is sufficient reason to attempt to understand it and also to seek ways to reduce its impact.

WHY ARE YOU IN SUCH A HURRY?

If you suffer from the time-pressure syndrome, let's ask the question, *Why are you in such a hurry?* The first answer that probably comes to mind is, "Because I've got so much to do." However, this answer, although superficially plausible, is off the mark and not very helpful.

Time pressure is perceived as objective, as external, and outside one's control. However, the fact of the matter is that it is caused by a negative *attitude*, a way of thinking about and behaving toward time that is self-defeating. Let's explore some of the factors involved in this attitude.

Age

The time-pressure syndrome is more characteristic of the somewhat older student than the younger student. Someone who is barely out of adolescence may feel that middle age and the retirement years exist in some remote, never-to-be-visited future. On the other hand, 31-year-old Barbara, referred to in the opening of this chapter, feels that time is running out. She thinks, "At the rate I'm going I'll be an old lady when I graduate from college."

The adult in college often thinks such thoughts as, "I've got to make up for lost time" or "I've only got a few good years left."

Taking On Too Much at Once

It would seem at first that taking on too much at once is an objective fact, that it is a *reality* that there is too much to do. However, it must be realized that taking on too much is a *decision*. In making out a class schedule the student thinks, "I'll take one more class. I can handle 12 units instead of 9." Or, in the role of parent, the individual thinks, "I know I could buy Susan a birthday cake from the store. But she loves the chocolate cake I make from scratch, and I've just *got* to do it for her." Clusters of decisions such as these place the individual in a psychological pressure cooker.

The crush of multiple responsibilities, many of them taken on by one's own decisions, make the person feel like Atlas carrying the world on inadequate shoulders.

Your Personality

One of the important aspects of one's personality is one's *temperament*, a natural tendency to react to various situations in a characteristic way. If your temperament is what is known as *phlegmatic*, you tend to be some-what relaxed and easy going, you eat well, and you enjoy life. Individuals with this kind of temperament are unlikely to suffer from the time-pressure syndrome. On the other hand, if your temperament is what is informally known as *high-strung*, you tend to be highly affected by your feelings, sober, aggressive, and tense. Individuals with this kind of temperament are more likely to suffer from the time-pressure syndrome.

Perfectionism

Perfectionism is the point of view that everything that one does must mea-sure up to a nearly impossible standard of excellence. Persons with the trait of perfectionism have ideas such as, "If it's worth doing, it's worth doing right" or "A sloppy job is a job half done." Although there is, of course, truth to these thoughts, the general approach can be taken to extremes. The individual is never quite satisfied. Nothing is ever good enough. It can be improved. Consequently, every task or project has to be done not just once but is done over several times. This takes up an inordinate amount of time and contributes to the time-pressure syndrome.

Students with the trait of perfectionism are never satisfied with a B in a class. They want an A. This is true even if the B will in no way damage them and will contribute toward their student careers. Consequently, such students often become compulsive studiers, devoting hours and hours to a review of material they already have learned to an acceptable standard.

Procrastination

Procrastination can play a significant role in the time-pressure syndrome. It is very common to avoid a task that is threatening or unpleasant. Common examples for students are putting off studying an assignment or writing a term paper. Procrastination is such a general problem that in informal surveys in my classes more than half of the students say that one of their bad habits is procrastination.

And yet common sense tells us that if we put off until tomorrow what we should do today we will end up in a time bind. Now a term paper that should have been worked on little by little over several weeks must be written in a few days. Or one finds oneself desperately cramming in a state of near-panic just before an important examination.

Procrastination is such an important problem that toward the end of this chapter a section is devoted to a key way to cope with the habit of putting off tasks.

THE ART OF TIME MANAGEMENT

Time management is an art. It takes intelligence and a conscious effort to manage time well. In the same way that a lawn that needs mowing won't mow itself, untended time won't keep itself in trim. You have to impose some sense of order on the days and the weeks. Think of the art of time management as learnable, and the more you do it the better you get at it. Below are some of the skills involved in time management.

- Reflect on your age. Take on a new attitude toward it. Instead of feeling that you must make up for lost time because you are an adult in college, think of yourself as comparatively young. Decide that there is "world enough and time" to accomplish your goals. To mix metaphors, the negative idea that one is "over the hill" is a kind of "crying over spilt milk." Decide that you are rich with future. I know a man who thought he would die at 39 because his father died of a heart attack at 39. Today that man is 82. I know of another man who retired from the post office at age 55. He went to medical school, became a physician, and practiced in a small town until he was 93. Just get rid of the idea that you are too old and that the specter of time is breathing down your neck. It's a false idea, and has no more reality than what you give it.

- Stop taking on too much at once. Decide to limit your responsibilities and lighten your burden. It is for good reason that the subtitle of this chapter is "Are you biting off more than you can chew?" Making a specific application to your student role, *never* take more classes than you can study for properly. In order to be fair to yourself, you need to allow, on average, five or six hours of study time per week for a given class. You need a master plan; there is more about this in the next section, "Making a Rational Schedule."

- Learn to cope with your own personality. If you are a high-strung type, and induce much of your own time pressure, decide that you don't have to be the victim of yourself. The ideas and suggestions in this chapter, if actually applied, can do much to modify the impact of your temperament in a positive way. Although it seems correct that temperament is to a large extent inborn, and consequently natural to the individual, it is also true that the *way* in which traits of temperament are expressed is learned. Never say, "Oh, well, what can I do? That's just me, that's the way I am and there's nothing I can do about it." You, your loved ones, and your academic work will all suffer if you insist on retaining this attitude. Instead, say, "I'm conscious, I can think, and I *can* change the way in which I habitually respond."

- Reject perfectionism. The philosopher Plato called this world—the Earthly world—an imperfect world. Only the Ideal World—a realm represented by God or Eternal Nature—is unchanging and perfect. Your day-to-day existence is in *this* world, the world of children with colds, cranky bosses, balky cars, and so forth. In view of the fact that nothing around you is absolutely perfect, decide that you have a right to be imperfect too. There *are* times to have high standards, to strive for excellence, but in order to protect your mental and emotional health there are also times to throw in the towel and say, "This is good enough." In many cases, a B or a C in a course may be "good enough." An A may not be required for your academic major. You may be wanting it in order to feed your pride. If so, recognize this, and also recognize that long-term success is seldom built on a foundation of impossible self-demands.

- If chronic procrastination is one of your problems, then you need to develop a strategy for coping with it. See the section near the end of the chapter called "Avoiding Procrastination."

- Learn to get an early start. If you normally set your alarm clock for 6:00 A.M., set it for 5:50. You won't miss the 10 minutes of sleep, but you will get rid of that rushed feeling. As a general principle, give yourself some extra time. Leave for school 10 minutes early. If you drive, you won't feel that you have to cut in and out of traffic in order to make up for lost time. Arrive at your classes one or two minutes early on a regular basis instead of one or two minutes late. Decide that the clock is your friend, not your enemy. If you start moving a little while before you actually have to, you will get rid of that feeling that you are always on the run. Getting an early start, something that is largely under your control, provides you with a time safety net.

- Assign priorities to your tasks. You may not be physically able to do everything you want to do, and it is important that you accept the fact that every *want* is not a *must*. Make an informal list of the three or four most important things that you want to accomplish in a given day. Take care of the most important item first, then go on to the second, and so forth. For example, if you have to study, you may have to wash the kitchen floor tomorrow or even the next day. It is important that you not feel guilty about tasks that you neglect for a few days because of more urgent demands.

MAKING A RATIONAL SCHEDULE

It is important that you make out a rational schedule, one designed to meet the needs of a typical week. A schedule allows you to see the whole week from a bird's-eye view and it makes it possible for you to find a *Gestalt*, a complete pattern or organized whole. This is very useful because it allows you to plan effectively and reduce details to their proper proportions. A schedule is, in effect, a time map; consequently, it is a very helpful guide.

In order to make out a schedule, take a standard unruled $8^{1}/_{2} \times$ 11-inch sheet of paper. Leaving a left-hand margin for times of day, across the top list the days of the week: Sunday, Monday, Tuesday, and so forth. Space them approximately one inch apart. Now proceed down the left-hand margin and list the times of day, starting with your normal getting-up time (e.g., 6:00 A.M., 7:00 A.M., 8:00 A.M., etc.). Space the times approximately three quarters of an inch apart. Let's say that you have allowed yourself 7 hours of sleep. This means you are awake 17 hours a day. Consequently, you should end up with a grid containing 17×7, or 119, time slots. Using a pencil, not a pen, write in a projection of how you intend to spend the major portion of a given hour. Here are some of the key words to use: Class, study, library, term paper, job, drive, shop, cook, children, recreation, socialize, and relax. The pencil, instead of a pen, is important because it allows you to work on your schedule and modify it as required.

Now look over your schedule. If you have signed up for, say, nine semester units, you should have also scheduled, if you are an average student, approximately 18 hours for study or other class-related activities. I realize that we're all individuals, and perhaps you can be an effective student if you allow half as much study time. On the other hand, don't kid yourself. Your schedule may reveal that in terms of your total responsibilities, you are biting off more than you can chew. If so, face reality and make some hard decisions. You may have to prune and clip here and there. In the end, of course, only you are the expert on your own life, and you must make the decisions. But the schedule will be an important analytical tool.

At least 10 percent or more of your schedule should allow you time for rest and relaxation. This will be approximately 10 to 12 hours a week. Don't protest that you haven't got the time. *You* are making the schedule, not Fate or the forces of nature. Modifying an old adage, remember, "All work and no play makes Jack and Jill into dull people."

Think of your schedule as an ideal, and attempt to approximate it. However, an approximation is not a perfect fit, merely a *near* fit. So don't be too hard on yourself if you can't meet the exact terms of the schedule. You are not a robot. Also, keep in mind that the schedule is not chiseled in stone; it is written in pencil. So feel free to modify it and shape it to your own personality.

I have referred to the schedule as a rational one. Let's focus on the word *rational*. This suggests that your schedule will be logical and reality oriented. It is something that you *can* do, not an impossible strait-jacket that leaves you exhausted and a bundle of nerves at the end of the week. A rational schedule is comfortable and loose-fitting. Make your schedule with these ideas in mind.

AVOIDING PROCRASTINATION

As noted earlier, procrastination can play a significant role in the time-pressure syndrome. It is a common bad habit. In this section, a specific method is applied to the tendency to put off studying and doing assignments. The method in question is called the *Premack principle,* and it was first formulated by David Premack, a learning theorist. (An informal name for the principle is the *Grandparent rule.*)

In brief, the Premack principle says this: Take note of any two behaviors in a person's set of common behaviors. Let's designate them Behavior A and Behavior B. Assume that Behavior A is not displayed very often on a spontaneous or voluntary basis, and assume that Behavior B is. It is possible to increase the frequency of occurrence of Behavior A by making it a way of obtaining the opportunity to engage in Behavior B. When this is done, the probability of occurrence of Behavior A goes up and the probability of occurrence of Behavior B goes down. That is the principle in its abstract form.

All of this may sound very theoretical and complex, but it is not. In practice it is very practical and straightforward. The Premack principle is often used in behavior modification applied to children. A child is asked to perform a task with a low probability of spontaneous occurrence, such as throwing out the trash, mowing the lawn, or studying. The child wants to watch television or call a friend on the telephone first. Applying the Premack principle, the parent says, "No. First you have to do your home-work. Then you can call Susan and talk." If you allow the child to engage in the high probability activity first, with no psychological strings attached, there will be more and more "goofing off" and less and less work done. (Now you know why the Premack principle is also called the Grandparent rule. It suggests an old-fashioned grandparent who will accept no non-sense or feeble excuses from children who want to get out of their chores.)

You can learn to treat yourself the way an effective parent, or grand-parent, treats a child. This is a part of the art of the *self-modification of behavior*, the application of principles of behavior modification to yourself. When you find yourself tempted to postpone studying or doing an assignment, make a well-defined behavioral contract with yourself. (You can do this mentally, but at first it might help to write down a key sentence or two.) First, clearly define the task such as, "study five pages," or "write three pages of my term paper," or "read ten pages toward my book report." Note that in defining the task you should define it in terms of the task itself, *not* time. If you define it in terms of time, thinking, "I'll study for an hour," you will tend to watch the clock and be impatient for time to pass. On the other hand, if you become *task-oriented*, instead of time-oriented, you will concentrate on the work to be done and time will pass quickly.

When you have completed the task, feel free to take a break and engage in one of your high probability behaviors. In practice, this will be something pleasant, something you look forward to, such as taking a walk, reading a few pages in a popular novel, socializing, and so forth. Take the break *even if in terms of your master schedule the time is allotted to study*. Again, this frees you from the perception that time functions like a straitjacket. It is important to actually *give yourself permission* to engage in the pleasant task. If you don't, thinking that you can move on directly to some other demanding task, your child self will feel cheated. Eventually it will rebel and resist, and you will find yourself going back to the procrastination habit.

The Premack principle is generally regarded as one of the most powerful tools in self-modification of behavior. Make a conscious effort to apply it, and you are likely to be pleased with the result.

CONCLUDING REMARKS

You don't have to suffer from the time-pressure syndrome. If you apply the methods explained in this chapter, you will find that you can eliminate much of the stress associated with a constellation of demands and responsibilities, and in turn you will be happier, healthier, and a more effective student.

To be a slave of time is, of course, foolish. The humorist Will Rogers recognized this when he said, "Half our life is spent trying to find something to do with the time we have rushed through life trying to save."

KEY POINTS TO REMEMBER

- *Time management* is a voluntary process in which specific skills are used to reduce stress and increase effectiveness by learning to budget time in a rational manner.
- The *time-pressure syndrome* consists of a set of negative and self-defeating attitudes and behaviors.
- The principal signs and symptoms of the time-pressure syndrome are: (1) Always being in a hurry, (2) a constant sense of urgency, (3) impatience, (4) hostility, and (5) doing two things at once.
- The terms *time-pressure syndrome* and *Type A behavior* have approximately the same meaning.
- Some of the key factors associated with the time-pressure syndrome are: (1) Your age, (2) taking on too much at once, (3) your personality, (4) perfectionism, and (5) procrastination.
- The chapter identifies a number of skills involved in time management. Six of these are: (1) Taking on a new attitude toward your chronological age, (2) deciding to limit your responsibilities, (3) learning to cope with your own personality, (4) rejecting perfectionism, (5) getting an early start, and (6) assigning priorities to tasks.
- A rational weekly schedule allows you to plan effectively and reduce details to their proper proportions.
- One way to avoid procrastination is to apply the *Premack principle* to your own behavior.

10

WRITING A TERM PAPER

"But I'm No Author!"

It is the first meeting of a U.S. History class. The professor announces the course requirements and mentions, almost casually, "Oh, by the way, a term paper will be required. It's due by the end of the semester. And you will receive an incomplete in the course if you don't turn it in."

You can almost hear a collective groan from the class. You yourself think, "But I'm no author! Maybe I should drop this class." All sorts of doubts and questions assail you.

If you are an adult in college, you may feel particularly threatened because you are rusty and have written nothing but a few letters to friends and notes to your spouse and children for a number of years. You look around at those who are younger than you and imagine that they are organized, creative, and competent. Nothing could be further from the truth! The fact of the matter is that a very large percentage of students, even relatively young ones just out of high school, lack the skills required to research and write a term paper. In fact, you, the responsible adult, possibly have the edge over the younger student because you are highly motivated and open to suggestion, will make your time count, and have a sincere, positive attitude. These factors more than compensate for the years you have been out of school.

FEELING LOST AND CONFUSED

It is not at all unusual for beginning college students to feel lost and confused when an instructor or professor announces that a term paper is required, because there is often a large gap between what the instructor assumes you know and what you actually know about writing papers. Let's help you bridge that gap by asking and answering a few basic questions:

What Is a Term Paper?

A term paper is a relatively long report or essay on a specific topic. It is submitted in order to satisfy a course requirement.

Why Are Term Papers Assigned at All?

Contrary to the grumbles and gripes to which we are all prone, the assignment of a term paper is *not* an effort on the part of an instructor to make you suffer and to engage in arbitrary harassment. A moment's reflection indicates that a term paper is an opportunity for you to display that you can make connections between concepts, do a little research, and express your thoughts in a clear form. This helps the instructor evaluate your grasp of the subject that he or she is teaching.

What Kinds of Courses Require Term Papers?

On the whole, you will find that term papers are likely to be required in social science and humanities courses. Examples of such courses include English literature, psychology, philosophy, anthropology, sociology, and history. A term paper is seldom required in life science or physical science courses such as biology, anatomy, physiology, astronomy, and physics. Also, term papers are seldom required in applied courses such as accounting, marketing, word processing, real estate, statistics, and business mathematics.

How Does a Term Paper Differ from a Thesis or a Dissertation?

A term paper is much shorter than a thesis or a dissertation, which tend to resemble book-length manuscripts. Like a term paper, they are also reports or essays. A thesis is submitted in order to satisfy one of the requirements for a master's degree, and a dissertation is submitted in order to satisfy one of the requirements for a doctoral degree.

But I've Heard that a Term Paper Must Have a Thesis. This is Kind of Confusing. Can You Clarify?

The term *thesis* can be used in two ways. To say that you are *writing* a thesis is to say that you are writing a long report or essay for a master's degree. To say that your term paper must *have* a thesis is to say that it must make a point, it must have some central idea. It is a good idea to set out this point or idea as a formal, explicitly stated proposition early in the paper. Then bring forth evidence that either supports or rejects the proposition. Show the pros and cons. Conclude by demonstrating that the bulk of your research supports the thesis.

For example, in a term paper for a U.S. History class your thesis might be: "The wild, wild West wasn't nearly as dangerous and lawless as we tend to think it was." Your paper might be called, "The Mild, Mild West." In order to support your thesis you would bring forth facts from articles and books showing that the vast bulk of early settlers in small towns in the western part of the United States were families and most people didn't carry guns. You would also cite shoot-outs and killings and bad men, but you would demonstrate that novels and movies have given these events an excessive importance. The concluding paragraphs of your term paper would try to convince the reader that the Old West was significantly less dangerous in terms of shooting and killings than some of today's big cities.

How Long Should a Term Paper Be?

If you ask a professor this question, you will often find that it is difficult to get a straight answer. Frequently the response will be something like, "As long as you think it needs to be to treat the subject fairly." If you do your research diligently, and collect a lot of facts and information, you may find yourself writing 30 or 40 pages. This is *too long* for a term paper; you are overwriting.

The instructor tends to gives you a devious answer because he or she wants you to think for yourself. Be that as it may, I will give you a straight answer. The ideal length for a term paper is the length of an average magazine article, about 3,000 to 3,500 words. In terms of typewritten pages, this is 12 to 14 pages. If you write much less, it will appear that you are slighting your topic. If you write much more, it will appear that you can't sort out relevant information from irrelevant information and have a poor ability to synthesize and organize ideas.

How Do You Find Information for a Term Paper?

Learn to use the library's reference resources. A card or computer catalog will list many subjects. Look up the subject you have picked and any subjects related to it and then find books and articles that contain facts and information associated with your topic. The indexes and bibliographies of the books and articles you first locate will often suggest other sources, and you can follow these leads. If your library doesn't have a particular publication, and you have time, you can often request it through an inter-library loan service. There are also helpful publications for researchers, such as *Books in Print* and *The Reader's Guide to Periodical Literature*. Additionally, there are annual abstracts published for some subjects, such as *Psychological Abstracts*.

Don't hesitate to approach a reference librarian for assistance. These individuals are trained in library science, are available at a convenient desk in most college libraries, and can sometimes accomplish in a few minutes what would take you hours. They are almost invariably helpful and courteous. This is their full-time occupation, and they *enjoy* showing you how to dig out facts and information.

It is important that you cite primary sources as well as secondary ones in a term paper. A *primary source* of information is a "first," or basic, source. An example of a primary source for a term paper on the Old West would be a biography written by a physician who actually treated several gunfighters. A *secondary source* of information is one that has been de-rived from primary ones. An example of a secondary source would be an encyclopedia article on the Old West. If you cite only the encyclopedia article, your professor will have little respect for your work because you are taking the easy way out. The author of the article has done the work that you were supposed to do.

How Do I Put a Term Paper into a Proper Form?

Obtain from the college bookstore a copy of *A Manual for Writers of Term Papers, Theses, and Dissertations*, which was originally written by Kate L. Turabian and was revised and expanded by Bonnie Birtwistle Honingsblum. It was first published in 1937, has gone through many editions, and is published by the University of Chicago Press. The manual will give you the key tips you need to know in order to make a table of contents, cite publications, organize a bibliography, and so forth. The bookstore will also have other good, standard manuals available.

FINDING A TOPIC

One of the principal problems you will encounter when assigned to write a term paper is finding a topic. The topic should have certain characteristics. First, it should not be too difficult to research. Second, it should have an aspect that you can state in the form of a thesis or a proposition. Third, it should not be too broad in scope. For example, in psychology a term paper on psychotherapy is too broad in scope. A term paper on a particular kind of psychotherapy, such as rational-emotive therapy, defines a limited territory of investigation. And fourth, the subject should excite some actual interest in you.

You will find in practice that the above criteria are not too difficult to meet. What is more difficult poses itself as a question: "How do I find *any* subject to write about?" Or, put differently, "How do I get an *idea* for a term paper?" The answer is not actually as difficult as you might think, and in reality is quite straightforward.

Open the course-assigned textbook to the index. (If there is no assigned textbook, find a standard textbook on the course's subject matter in the library.) Let's say that you are trying to find a topic in psychology. You will find between 600 to 1,000 entries in the index. It is no exaggeration to say that at least one-fourth of these would make good term-paper topics. In order to make my point, I have picked out a few from *only* the A entries in a standard textbook: Agoraphobia, Amnesia, Anorexia nervosa, Anxiety, Archetypes, Assertiveness training, Authoritarian personality, Autoerotic activity, and Autonomy. Any of these could form the core of a good psychology term paper.

Read the textbook entry for the subject, and that is your starting point. Use it as a stimulus for your own thought processes. Ask yourself how you could make an interesting statement or proposition about the topic, one that could be answered to some extent by library research. For example, let's say that you look up *autonomy* and learn that B. F. Skinner, an eminent behavioral psychologist, argued that human beings have no genuine autonomy, no real freedom of choice. On the other hand, you learn that Abraham Maslow, a founder of humanistic psychology, asserted that the capacity to make real choices is a given of the human condition. Let's say that you side with Maslow. Your thesis could be: "In spite of impersonal factors such as genetics and environment, human beings have actual autonomy." Then your research focuses on information that sheds some light on the proposition.

USING THE FOUR STAGES OF CREATIVE THINKING

Researchers have discovered that there are four basic stages in creative thinking. And make no mistake about it, writing a term paper is a creative project. The four stages are: (1) preparation, (2) incubation, (3) illumination, and (4) verification. Let's see how we can apply the four stages in order to produce an actual term paper.

For a concrete example, let's return to our term paper called "The Mild, Mild West" in which we assert that the Old West wasn't as wild as it has been said to have been.

Preparation

Perhaps, to get in the mood, you read two or three Western novels by such authors as Zane Grey, Max Brand, or Louis L'Amour. Then, using the library's resources, you find books and articles on the way people lived approximately 100 years ago in such states as Texas, Arizona, Nevada, and California. Read only the material that is pertinent to your topic. Use the bibliographies of the first books you consult to suggest additional books and articles.

Take plenty of notes on the material you read. It is helpful to put these on index cards of a standard size so that you can easily arrange and re-arrange your material. Also, make photocopies of key pages.

Let's say that you have collected information over a period of two or three weeks. You have a pile of material, and it seems both random and chaotic. You look at it in despair and wonder how you'll ever get it organized. It is at exactly this point that Step 2, Incubation, becomes important.

Incubation

Set aside your notes for a period of time—for example, a week or two. Incubation in creative thinking is a mental process involving learning and growth at a subconscious level. Although you do not give conscious attention to the subject matter, apparently some process of connecting between facts and ideas goes on outside your voluntary control. It is a very real phenomenon, one you can count on, and one you need to take advantage of.

Note that *time* is involved, however. In the example I have given, work on the term paper, including preparation and incubation, has been spread out over a three- to four-week period. For this reason, it is important to get an early start and not procrastinate when you have been assigned a term paper to write.

Illumination

After the incubation period, come back to the material. You will be pleasantly surprised to find that it tends to organize itself easily and that you have some good ideas about how to write it up.

For example, you see that a gunfight from a Western novel can be quoted briefly in an introduction. This gets the paper off to an interesting start. The following topical headings come naturally to mind: (1) The Popular View, (2) A Realistic View, (3) An Evaluation, and (4) A Personal Viewpoint. You need no more than four or five major headings for a term paper. Three or four pages of writing under each heading will give you all the total pages you need.

Verification

The last step in the creative process involves sitting down and actually writing the term paper. You are verifying your ideas and your organization, turning mental musings into actual sentences and paragraphs on paper. Keep in mind that verification is a trial-and-error process. It is for good reason that a first draft is also called a *rough draft*. The key goal is to produce a document. After something is down on paper, it is relatively easy to go back over it two or three times, editing, rewriting, and improving the paper.

It may be helpful to conceptualize the process of verification in the following way. You do the actual writing from your child self, a side of your personality that is spontaneous and creative. Don't do much self-criticism or editing while writing the first draft. You do the evaluation and rewriting from your adult self, a side of your personality that is rational and logical.

If you employ the four stages of creative thinking as outlined, you will find that you can actually produce a term paper of high quality with a minimum of psychological pain and suffering.

SPECIFIC TIPS AND WRITING STRATEGIES

Think of the following specific tips and writing strategies as a checklist. You may not be able to incorporate all of the items on the list simultaneously as you are writing the rough draft of your paper, but when you are rewriting and editing, you can go over the paper with the checklist as a guide.

- Start your paper with an example, a quotation, or an anecdote that is intrinsically interesting and attention getting. This helps to lift your paper out of the morass of dull and uninspired term papers your instructor plows through at the end of each semester. Remember that an instructor is like any reader, and you want to do everything in your power to engage his or her spontaneous attention. However, after you have the reader's attention, settle down. Don't use too many anecdotes or other attention-getting material, or your paper will not be seen as scholarly but merely as a cute and superficial effort.

- Keep the writing clear and to the point. Use relatively short sentences ranging in length from 10 to 14 words. If a sentence has too many clauses and subclauses, and approaches a length of 20 or more words, break it down into two shorter sentences. Use a vocabulary that is appropriate to your subject, but don't indulge in fake erudition by employing obscure words when more familiar, workable words will do. You won't impress the instructor at all by taking a heavy-handed, overly abstract approach to your writing.

- Use headings and subheadings. As indicated earlier, give your term paper about four or five main headings. If the material under a heading lends itself to ready categorization, then use some subheadings. Remembering the basic rules of outlining, be sure that you have at least two subheadings, if you use them at all, under a main heading. The use of headings and subheadings gives your paper the appearance of being logical and organized. Twelve pages of writing without headings can sometimes look like a big lump of indigestible mental oatmeal.

- Limit your references. You really don't have to go overboard on research for a term paper. Remember, it is not a thesis or a dissertation. How many references is the right number? As a rough rule of thumb, think in terms of an average of one per page. Consequently, if your term paper is 12 pages in length, then 10 to 14 references will be about right. If you have too few references, your paper will not appear to be adequately documented. If you have too many references, your paper will seem to be cluttered and written from index cards. The important point is to be sure you rely mainly on *primary* references of high quality.

- Summarize all references in a bibliography. Although this is basic information given in all standard term-paper manuals, I want to reiterate it with special emphasis because I have seen more than one term paper turned in without a bibliography or with a bibliography sloppily done. A bibliography is a real showcase for your research. It is often the first item an instructor turns to, so be sure that it is neat, accurate, and presented in correct form; this will really help to move your paper up your professor's grading scale.

- Edit the paper carefully. Double-check and triple-check your paper for spelling errors, grammar, and general syntax. If you need help in this regard, have someone else do some basic editing. This is called *copyediting*, and it is not unethical unless the other individual begins to do some actual writing and makes a creative contribution to the paper.

- Pay attention to the paper's general appearance. A whole grade point can often be gained or lost on a term paper because of its overall look. Some papers are turned in typed on faded, overused ribbons. Others are turned in run off from old dot-matrix printers, and the print has a grainy look. In contrast, it is better to use a crisp, carbon ribbon. A dot-matrix printer is acceptable if the resolution is high. The best look is obtainable with the use of a laser printer. If you don't have adequate equipment, it is possible to have your paper copied and run off at a modest cost by a professional service. Think of Eliza Doolittle in *My Fair Lady* going to the ball. The royalty think she is a lady of high quality because of the way she is dressed and the way she presents herself. Your term paper is more likely to be judged of high quality if it is dressed properly.

- Use some direct quotations. Direct quotations, properly referenced, lend weight and authority to your paper. Be sure that they are interesting, insightful, and pertinent to the content. However, a little goes a long way, so don't overdo it. And don't string two or three quotes together; they tend to lose their luster when this is done. Three or four quotations, here and there, in a standard-length term paper, are about the right number.

- Remember that writing is rewriting. As indicated earlier, write the first draft relatively rapidly from the child side of your personality. Rewrite and edit at your leisure from the adult side of your personality. I am repeating this suggestion here for emphasis because it is extremely important.

CONCLUDING REMARKS

Have confidence in yourself. You may object, "This is easier said than done!" By applying the methods detailed in this chapter, however, you can overcome many of your doubts. The systematic approach described will both reduce your anxiety and provide you with the assurance that you are treading on firm ground. And you *will* produce a competent term paper.

Remember that as an adult in college you have a little more wisdom and a little more maturity than you had a few years ago. This will shine through almost automatically in any term paper you write.

KEY POINTS TO REMEMBER

- A term paper is a relatively long report or essay on a specific topic.
- Term papers are assigned in order to provide you with an opportunity to display that you can make connections between concepts, do a little research, and express your thoughts in a clear form.
- A term paper should have a thesis. In other words, it must make a point; it must have some central idea. It is a good idea to set out this point or idea as a formal, explicitly stated proposition early in the paper.
- The ideal length of a term paper is 12 to 14 typewritten pages.
- A *primary source* of information is a "first," or basic, source. A *secondary source* is one that has been derived from primary ones.
- Use the index of a standard textbook to find term paper topics.
- Apply the four stages of creative thinking in order to produce a term paper. The four stages are: (1) preparation, (2) incubation, (3) illumination, and (4) verification.
- Start your paper with an example, a quotation, or an anecdote that is intrinsically interesting and attention getting.
- Keep the writing clear and to the point.
- Use headings and subheadings.
- Edit the paper carefully.
- Pay attention to the paper's general appearance.
- Use some direct quotations.
- Remember that writing is rewriting.

11

PUBLIC SPEAKING

The Number-One Fear of Most Students

Carl L., age 28, is a meter reader for a power company, married, and the father of two children. He is taking evening classes at a local community college, and he hopes to earn a degree in electronic engineering. This semester he is enrolled in an English literature class, and he has been given the assignment of presenting a 10-minute oral book report on George Orwell's *1984*. Every student in the class has to give an oral book report on a novel selected from a list of recommended books. There are many moans and groans and fears expressed by the students to each other when they are on break and out of earshot of the instructor:

"I don't know why we have to give oral reports. Isn't a written report good enough?"

"When I have to give a talk before a group, my mind goes blank."

"I hope I can read my report word for word. If the teacher allows that, I can get through it."

Carl says, "This assignment is definitely not my kind of thing. In high school whenever I gave an oral report my mouth went dry and my pulse seemed to double. I really think that this kind of requirement is unnecessary. What good is public speaking going to do me as an electronic engineer?" It's been 10 years since Carl has given a talk to a class or group of any kind, and he's thinking a host of self-defeating and anxiety-arousing thoughts.

Carl and his fellow students are not alone. It has been said that public speaking is the number-one college-related fear of most students. Many students instantly drop a class when an oral presentation is required. If a course in public speaking is a graduation requirement, the course is often seen as a major stumbling block and is avoided until there are no options left. Worse yet, a few really fearful souls never take the course and, consequently, never graduate.

Before we proceed, let's explore the positive side of public speaking. What benefits will accrue to you if you develop any ability at all to give a presentation in front of a group? Here are three:

1. *A gain in self-confidence.* If you can overcome your anxiety and your resistance, and can learn to make an effective presentation, you will find a substantial rise in your overall sense of competence. Positive experiences rub off on your whole personality and tend to give you a lift.

2. *A decrease in general anxiety.* People who learn to speak in public sometimes find that by mastering one fear, the fear of appearing before an audience, that they can often master other fears. Assertive behavior, even if displayed by an effort of will at first, feeds back on itself and helps to regulate vague apprehensions.

3. *An improvement in mental organization.* The skills and disciplines involved in saying something interesting and to the point in a relatively short time tend to help you to facilitate both clear thinking and the capacity to lay out plans.

The two primary situations in college that will require public speaking have already been referred to above, (1) making oral reports and (2) taking a public-speaking class. As indicated, these two are associated with a class or school *requirement.* However, there are situations in which *voluntary* public speaking may be a factor. If you join a club or become active in student government, then public-speaking skills will also be of value to you.

Subsequently, in the vocation of your choice, you will find that the ability to speak in public is important. Carl L. is wrong if he thinks that electronic engineers need only be competent in their specialized professional work. Those who are the rising stars in companies are often the ones who can make effective presentations to groups of fellow engineers. Also, the effective speaker can help the company sell a product to prospective buyers.

If you hope to go into private practice one day as a physician, dentist, accountant, psychologist, marriage and family counselor, attorney, or similar service-related occupation, you will find that you can acquire a clientele quickly by giving talks to local clubs, civic organizations, and other groups.

There isn't much doubt about it—the ability to speak in public is a valuable personal asset.

THE SPOTLIGHT PHENOMENON

You are standing before a class of students. All eyes are upon you. Your heart is pounding and your palms are moist. This is the *spotlight phenomenon*, a rise in anxiety level when one is the object of attention of a group or an audience. It is a natural psychological event and one to be expected in people who do very little public speaking.

The causes of the spotlight phenomenon are not mysterious, and they are easy enough to understand. In the first place, it may make you feel a little better to realize that the spotlight phenomenon is related, to some extent, to intelligence. It is a sign that you are sensitive and aware to feel anxiety when others are apparently evaluating you. Infants and toddlers cannot experience the spotlight phenomenon because they do not have a sufficiently developed awareness. They are too young to be self-conscious. On the other hand, pre-schoolers can and do experience the spotlight phenomenon because they *know* they are being looked at. Shyness also is associated with this developmental period. (The pre-school stage begins at around age 3.)

Another causal factor in the spotlight phenomenon is a bipolar personality trait known as *extraversion-introversion*. All of us have varying combinations of both traits or we couldn't function. However, some people seem to be born extraverts. They *like* the spotlight, and they don't mind being looked at. Such people take to public speaking like ducks take to water.

On the other hand, some people seem to be born introverts. They really have a *distaste* for the spotlight. They find it very disconcerting to be looked at. Freud, the father of psychoanalysis, seems to have been something of an introvert. One of the reasons he had patients recline on a couch, look away from him, and free-associate is because he said that he couldn't stand to be looked at all day long. And yet, in spite of his introverted tendencies, Freud was an accomplished public speaker.

Being perhaps more sensitive, reflective, and thoughtful than others, introverted persons tend to be acutely aware that they are being constantly evaluated and judged by an audience. Even if your tendencies are in the introverted direction, you can compensate and develop reasonable effectiveness as a public speaker.

AGGRAVATING FACTORS

Certain factors aggravate the spotlight phenomenon. And in order to help you understand and overcome it, it will be helpful to detail some of the key factors at this point.

1. *The idea that others are already effective speakers.* It is a common human tendency to think that everyone else is competent in an area where we experience a deficiency. Consequently, there is the false perception that all of the other students in the class will give smooth, glowing, fluent reports. And you will be the only fool.

2. *Poor body image.* Many of us, perhaps the majority, have a doubtful body image. We think we are too fat or too skinny, too tall or too short. You may think you have a big nose or bad skin. Giving a talk intensifies these self-perceptions, and you imagine that others are staring at you and silently laughing at you.

3. *Lack of preparation.* Although it seems an obvious error, it is amazing how many students make inadequate preparations for an oral presentation. They have not made a careful analysis for a book report or they don't have enough information for a talk on a subject. They have not adequately reviewed and rehearsed the talk. They don't have concise, useful notes. They have tried to memorize, but have remembered only half.

4. *Anxiety-arousing thoughts.* Often students think such thoughts as, "I will die if they laugh at me." or "I can't stand it when I bore people." Anxiety-arousing thoughts tend to convert the potential for a small failure into a great catastrophe.

5. *The belief that the speech must be perfect.* There is often the underlying idea: "I can't make any mistakes." There is the notion that the talk or speech must be a "hit"; otherwise it is a complete "miss." This is either-or thinking, and it is a logical error that resides behind a perfectionistic approach.

6. *Avoiding public speaking.* When you avoid a speaking assignment or a speech class, you experience a reduction in anxiety. Great! Or, maybe not so great. The reduction in anxiety reinforces the avoidance behavior and then strengthens it. Consequently, it is likely to be repeated in the future. The more you avoid, the more you will continue to avoid. It is a downward spiral.

7. *Lack of experience.* You, like most people, have probably had very little experience with making oral presentations. It is completely normal to feel a relatively high level of anxiety when you are asked to perform a complex task under these conditions.

8. *The "blank" mind.* A nagging thought that many people have just before they are to give a talk is: "My mind is going to go completely blank." An image comes to mind of a ventriloquist's dummy moving its jaw with no sound coming out. It's a frightening mental picture.

USING SOME CLEAR THINKING

The principal way to reduce the anxiety associated with those factors that aggravate the spotlight phenomenon is to apply some clear thinking to them. You need to look at each factor in a rational way. The idea here is not to get rid of *all* anxiety. *Moderate* anxiety is motivating and will have a positive effect on your performance. You just want to reduce your anxiety to a level where you can function, give your oral presentation, and not run away from the situation entirely.

Let's go over the list presented in the previous section item by item.

Item 1. *The idea that others are already effective speakers.* Most of the other students in the class are just as anxious and nervous about public speaking as you are. They are no more competent, fluent, organized, or intelligent than you are. They are sitting there thinking that you have the skills that they don't have.

Item 2. *Poor body image.* Just look around you at the other people in the class. Do they have perfect bodies? Are they all possessed of movie star faces? The odds are that you don't look much better or worse than the average of the lot. Although this may not be wonderful, it really ought to be good enough to keep you from feeling embarrassed when you stand up. They won't laugh at you just for being your natural self.

Item 3. *Lack of preparation.* This is something completely within your control. *Decide* to prepare fully and completely. Be well informed. Make good notes. But don't write out the talk word for word. Audiences seldom enjoy being read to. They like to feel that you are talking *with* them and developing your thoughts, to some extent, on the spot. You can rehearse by giving your talk to a friend or an empty room.

I *don't* recommend the old advice of giving your talk in front of a mirror. It will make you too self-conscious, you will see all of your flaws, and it may even aggravate your anxiety. For the same reasons, I don't recommend making either an audio tape or a videotape of yourself rehearsing the speech. These techniques may be employed in some public-speaking classes, but they should be used only under the supervision of a qualified instructor.

Item 4. Challenge anxiety-arousing thoughts with questions designed to deflate them. Ask yourself, "Will I really *die* if they laugh at me?" An example of the kind of logical answer that will come back to you in your own mind is, "Well, of course not. I may feel a little lousy, or a little depressed, but that's all. I can still go home after class. Nobody will lock me out. I can still sleep in my own bed." Voluntary self-oriented challenges will help you realize that you, like all people, are entitled to small failures if and when they do occur.

Item 5. *The belief that the speech must be perfect.* It is unrealistic to expect that your speech will be perfect. It is all right to make mistakes. In fact, there is *no other way* to give a talk. Even the world's most accomplished speakers make mistakes, engage in redundancies, correct themselves, have lapses, and so forth. Your speech isn't a complete "miss" if it is not a complete "hit." You only have to be somewhere in the vicinity of the target. Remember, you are being evaluated against other students, not polished public speakers.

Item 6. *Avoiding public speaking.* As already indicated, avoiding public speaking will only make matters worse for you in the long run. It is better to muster whatever courage you have and face reality. If you will yourself to go through with oral presentations, and not drop classes when they are required, you will desensitize yourself to the experience. Talking before a group will become less and less threatening.

Item 7. *Lack of experience.* You really can't help it if you lack experience. It's not you fault. Every person proficient in anything was a beginner once. Look at it this way: Even the great dancer Fred Astaire was at some point in his life a toddler who stumbled and fell as he took his first steps. Just say to yourself, "The only way to gain experience in public speaking is to experience public speaking." (This isn't as circular as it sounds.)

Item 8. *The "blank" mind.* It is highly unlikely that your mind will go completely blank and that you will remember *nothing*. After all, you have your notes, your key words, an outline, or *something* in your hand. If you have reviewed and rehearsed your material, most of it will come back to you with the stimuli available in your notes. The fear that you will have a "blank" mind is really the fear that you won't remember *everything*, that you will forget some of your best material. Although this can and does happen, it's not all that serious. Your listeners won't know you forgot because they didn't know what you were going to say.

MAKING AN ORAL PRESENTATION

I propose at this point to pass on to you a few tips that will improve almost any talk or oral presentation. These suggestions are based on quite a bit of public speaking experience on my part—I was an academic instructor in the Air Force; I put myself through graduate school in psychology by giving lectures on real-estate law; I have promoted my books by giving talks to groups; and I have been a college instructor for 30 years.

I offer these tips with some disquiet. I am concerned that if you make too much of a conscious effort to apply them, they will raise your anxiety level. And most of my effort in this chapter has been in the direction of lowering your anxiety level. Consequently, I am going to advise you to apply only one or two of the tips to a given talk. If you try to apply all of them simultaneously to your first few presentations, you will feel like a juggler with about nine balls in the air all at once.

1. *Have an attention-getting introduction.* Try to think of some way to "hook" an audience. A humorous remark is often effective, but it doesn't have to be a joke. An anecdote, a clever quotation, a news item, or a reference to a celebrity are all examples of material that have interest built into them.

2. *Make eye contact.* Don't talk to the floor, the lectern, your notes, or the back wall. Talk to people. The way in which people know that you are talking to them is to make eye contact. Don't make eye contact with just one person. On the other hand, you don't have to make eye contact with each and every member of the group. Use the principle of *roving eye contact.* Make it, hold it for 20 or 30 seconds, and then move on to someone else at random. Make sure that you include people at the back of the room. By the way, you will be able to tell if your audience is interested and attentive by the kind of eye contact they make with you.

3. *Use a visual aid or a handout.* Either of these provides a focal point for your talk. Frankly, they are psychological crutches, but

they will go a long way toward making you both more comfortable and more effective. Much of the information you want to convey can be contained in the aid or handout. A visual aid can be a large, prepared drawing or chart, or it can simply be information placed on a chalkboard.

A handout can be an either an outline of your talk or a list of key questions that you plan to address. Members of an audience tend to cling to handouts. I see them clutched during talks as if they were treasures (although they will probably be thrown away ten minutes later).

4. *Speak so you can be heard.* If you don't do anything else right, at least do this. An inaudible talk is no talk at all. Some students insist on giving a talk in soft, whispery tones. This can, of course, come from anxiety. However, it may also arise from the mistaken idea that modesty is becoming. It is *not* becoming when you are *supposed to be* the center of attention. Will yourself to speak up. A little too loud is better than a little too quiet. A low-volume presentation says implicitly, "What I have to say isn't worth hearing."

5. *Make some movements.* You are not a statue; you are in fact alive and breathing. Prove it by taking a few steps forward, or back, once in a while. Change your position. Come out from behind the lectern for a few moments. Walk over to the blackboard. Point at your visual aid. Motion automatically commands attention. It involuntarily makes all eyes focus on the body in motion and brings the audience together.

6. *Use natural hand gestures.* This is controversial advice. One school of thought takes the position that "talking with your hands" is rather "low" and "crude." This seems to me to be a rather out-of-date idea associated with an attitude that is completely out of tune with our democratic society.

The second school of thought takes the position that hand gestures naturally augment what we have to say. The appropriate "hand language" that comes naturally to you from your cultural background gives color and personality to what you have to say.

Now you have the answer to an old question asked by public-speaking students: "What do I do with my hands?" My answer is: "Use them." Alternatively, my answer could be: "Forget about them at a conscious level, and let them be spontaneously expressive."

7. *Use a key-questions format.* One very easy way to organize a talk is to draw up a series of four to seven key questions. Read the first question to the group, then look up and answer the question informally. Proceed through the other questions in the same way.

One alternative is to write the questions (not all at once) on the chalkboard. This will place you in automatic motion. A second alternative is to have the questions listed on a handout. This is a good alternative, but be careful that you do not put down more questions than you can answer. If you don't get to all of the questions on the handout, the audience will feel cheated. A better strategy is to leave out a few questions on the handout. If you have time, you can present a few more questions from your notes.

This method can be used for almost any kind of report or talk. For example, for the oral book report on George Orwell's *1984* the questions could be: (1) Who was George Orwell? (2) What is the basic plot of *1984*? (3) What is the basic point of the book? (4) Why do many people think that *1984* is a great book? (5) What is my own personal evaluation of *1984*? The problem with a format like this is not that you won't have enough material, but that you will make your answers too long and run overtime. Limit yourself to short, to-the-point answers.

For a talk on schizophrenia in a psychology class, here are examples of the kinds of key questions that might be asked: (1) What is schizophrenia? (2) What are its signs and symptoms? (3) Is it inherited or acquired? (4) Does it respond better to drugs or psychotherapy? (5) What percentage of people are victims of schizophrenia?

The key-questions format is effective because questions automatically alert the mind and induce a natural interest.

8. *Talk with feeling.* It is common to hear some students deliver a talk in a dull monotone. Often their faces seem to go blank and they lack expression. Conversely, other students vary the pitch of their voices. Their eyes and facial expression convey feeling, a degree of emotional intensity. The content of two talks can be almost the same, but the one delivered with feeling and liveliness will go over far better with an audience.

   It should not be a great effort to do this. On the contrary, the effort will probably go into suppressing your natural enthusiasm. Many students, hoping to gain the approval of their peers, give talks in a minimal, self-effacing manner. Not only will your peers fail to enjoy your presentation, but you will not earn the approval of the instructor, the only person evaluating you in the classroom who really counts. Let your personality express itself.

9. *Allow a little time for a question-and-answer period.* It is always gracious and a courtesy to invite some questions from the audience. It also conveys the impression that you are the master of your

material. No more than two or three questions need to be accepted. The quality of your answers is really not as important as the confidence with which you present them. Keep your answers relatively short. And, remember, in a question-and-answer format, you have a right to the last word. In your momentary role as speaker, you are the authority on the subject in question.

CONCLUDING REMARKS

The essayist and philosopher Ralph Waldo Emerson wrote, "All the great speakers were bad speakers at first." This observation suggests that the art of public speaking is just that, an *art*. And an art consists of a set of learnable skills. You can learn to develop a certain proficiency in speaking before groups. What is required is a will, applied intelligence, and practice.

KEY POINTS TO REMEMBER

- Three direct benefits to be gained by developing an ability to give a presentation in front of a group are: (1) A gain in self-confidence, (2) a decrease in general anxiety, and (3) an improvement in mental organization.
- In the vocation of your choice, you will often find that it is important to be able to speak in public.
- The *spotlight phenomenon* is a rise in anxiety level when one is the object of attention of a group or an audience.
- A basic cause of the spotlight phenomenon is the acute self-consciousness associated with knowing that we are being evaluated and judged by others.
- Eight factors aggravate the spotlight phenomenon. Three of these are: (1) The idea that others are already effective speakers, (2) anxiety-arousing thoughts, and (3) the belief that the speech must be perfect.
- Clear thinking applied to each of the aggravating factors can rob them of much of their negative power.
- There are at least nine ways to improve almost any talk or oral presentation. Four of these are: (1) Have an attention-getting introduction, (2) use a visual aid or a handout, (3) use natural hand gestures, and (4) use a key-questions format.

12

TAKING EXAMS

Some Practical Tips

Recently I asked a group of students to complete a sentence beginning with these words: "When I take an exam, I. : . . ."

Some of the responses I received included:

"When I take an exam, I don't usually do my best because I'm too nervous."

"When I take an exam, I feel naked, exposed. It's as if someone has stripped my personality of its psychological clothes."

"When I take an exam, I say to myself, 'Who are teachers to judge me?' I'm older than a lot of them."

"When I take an exam, I think that this is kid stuff. After all I've been through—three children and a divorce—it seems to be ridiculous to be sitting in a room scratching away at multiple-choice questions."

Many of the answers indicate that feelings of anxiety, confusion, and dislike of being judged are common. Among students who are over 25, frequently expressed feelings include (1) the notion that age in and of itself makes one a less competent test taker, (2) resentment toward instructors who are youthful, and (3) rancor based on the observation that examinations tend to look for specific knowledge, ignoring one's general wisdom, maturity, and life experience.

Very few completed sentences suggest that examinations are an *opportunity* to display one's learning and a *challenge* to one's intelligence and creativity.

Well, like it or not, positive attitude or no, examinations are a fact of life in college. Somehow they must be gotten through. So let's take a neutral attitude, let's just say, as great mountain climbers say, that the big piles of rocks are *there*. Examinations are one of the natural obstacles of academic life. And if you would like to climb to the peaks containing promising certificates, degrees, and rewarding careers, then you need to learn to cope effectively with examinations.

In Chapter 5 I described study methods that will help you prepare properly for examinations. Consequently, I will assume that you have studied effectively and are well prepared as you approach an examination. In this chapter I will analyze the basic nature of multiple-choice and essay questions, two common kinds. And I will provide practical methods and tips that will help you earn better scores.

TEST ANXIETY

If you commonly experience test anxiety, you are not alone. A majority of students, when interviewed or asked to fill out questionnaires, confess to some degree of test anxiety. It is normal to respond with fear, worry, and apprehension when you are threatened. And, make no mistake, you are threatened to some extent when you are asked to take an examination. If you are a serious, goal-oriented student, a lot is at stake when you are being evaluated. A pattern of low scores and failures can turn dreams to ashes.

In the vast majority of cases you won't be able to rid yourself of all anxiety, nor do you need to. As I have said earlier, moderate anxiety has actually been found to *facilitate* test performance. It motivates you, brings optimal psychological arousal, and helps you to maintain focused attention. Anxiety is a little distressing, but you should just decide that you *can* tolerate it. Taking an antianxiety drug will make you more comfortable, of course, but may take an important edge off your capacity to perform. Therefore, I *don't* recommend such drugs as a general way of coping with everyday examination jitters.

If your anxiety seems to you to be excessive and chronic, then it can, of course, be disruptive and interfere with good examination performance. Explore the anxiety-reduction methods in Chapter 8, the chapter on math anxiety, under the heading "Specific Antianxiety Strategies." Several of these can be readily adapted to any kind of examination, not only those in mathematics. If your own resources seem inadequate, seek help in the Counseling Office. Many colleges have counseling psychologists on their staffs who can help you acquire anxiety-reduction skills.

THE NATURE OF MULTIPLE-CHOICE QUESTIONS

A multiple-choice question challenges learning by invoking a memory retrieval process called *recognition*. A parallel process, the one invoked by essay and short-answer fill-in-the-blank questions, is called *recall*.

Of the two processes, recognition is considered the less demanding one because the stimuli required for the memory are manifest, they are presented right in front of your eyes. Recall, on the other hand, requires the dredging up of information from a memory storage level to the conscious level.

Let's say that a history question is posed as follows: "Who was the President of the United States during World War I?"

Now pose the same basic question in the following manner:

The president of the United States during World War I was:

a. Harry S Truman
b. Franklin Delano Roosevelt
c. Woodrow Wilson
d. Herbert Hoover

It is obvious that, if you have any memory of the correct answer at all, you are more likely to get it right if presented with the multiple-choice format as opposed to the short-answer format. Asked a direct question requiring recall, you may be unable to think of the answer. You say, "It's on the tip of my tongue."

The tip-of-the-tongue phenomenon, one that has been studied by educational psychologists, suggests that some of the information in memory exists in a kind of memory twilight zone. It *is* learned, it *is* remembered, but barely. Therefore, it needs a boost, or a stepping stool, to get it up and out of memory. The multiple-choice test provides such a boost.

To some extent, the thrust of the above paragraphs has been to lead you to the understanding that when instructors give you multiple-choice questions, they are, to a large extent, doing you a favor. They are presenting information to you in such a way that if you have learned it at all, not even too well, you have some chance at success. There is a tendency among students to bad-mouth multiple-choice tests. Sometimes they are called, with a negative connotation, "Multiple-guess tests."

It is all well and good to act as if one is above multiple-choice tests, to imply that they are impersonal and mechanical, to indicate that they reward guessing, to suggest that they don't reveal creative abilities, and so forth. But what is the alternative? The only major testing alternative in content-oriented classes are essay examinations. And the vast majority of students dislike these more than they dislike multiple-choice questions. So hesitate and reflect before you heap verbal abuse on the mule of academic testing, the multiple-choice test.

From the instructional point of view, one of the main advantages of multiple-choice tests is that they allow for objective grading. On a typical mid-semester examination there might be 50 questions. Using a mask with punched-out holes over a standard answer sheet provided by the student, a test can be graded in as little as 10 to 20 seconds. In many colleges the instructor can send the answer sheet to a computer center for machine grading. Large numbers of students can be quickly and reliably tested.

The instructor can then assign a grading scale to the scores. On an absolute scale, it is common to assign As to those who obtain 100 percent to 90 percent correct, Bs to those who obtain 90 percent to 80 percent correct, and so forth. On the other hand, if this absolute scale is too harsh, then the instructor may decide to grade on the curve. The purpose of the curve is to make allowances for individual differences and/or for the fact that the test might have been too difficult, or inappropriate in some way, for the group. A curve is assigned based on an instructor's convictions and assumptions. One example of a commonly used curve is to assign As to the top 10 percent of scores in a group. (If a hundred students take the test, there will be 10 As.) The next 20 percent receive Bs. The next 40 percent receive Cs. The next 20 percent receive Ds. The bottom 10 percent receive Fs. This sums to 100 percent and is nicely balanced. It also provides that a total of 70 percent of the class will pass with a C or better.

Some students protest that this curve is unfair, that it automatically dooms some students to the D or F category. This is seldom the way in which the described curve is applied. It is usually applied in such a way that only if students fall below *two* criteria, imposed by *both* an absolute standard and the curve, will they receive a D or an F. The truth of the matter is that the curve is often used to give the student the benefit of the doubt.

A multiple-choice examination is actually a fairly good way to assess the acquisition of basic information. It is not a good way, however, to assess your capacity to integrate concepts, to make complex connections among ideas, and to think creatively. If the instructor wants to assess these aspects of learning, then it is necessary to turn to essay examinations.

THE NATURE OF ESSAY QUESTIONS

As indicated earlier, the memory process invoked by essay and short-answer fill-in-the-blank questions is called *recall*. Recall places a much greater demand on the memory process than does recognition because the answer is not manifest. It is nowhere to be seen in the objective world, and it must be produced for a blank sheet of paper by the mind itself.

Short-answer fill-in-the-blank questions are sometimes called "short essay" questions because they, like large-scope essay questions, demand a recall process. However, the purpose of short questions is usually to assess the acquisition of terms, concepts, and key information. This is not the primary purpose of an essay question.

The primary purpose of an essay question is to assess your capacity to *tie together*, or *make connections* among, terms, concepts, and key pieces of information. In educational psychology this process is usually called *critical thinking*. Consequently, more is demanded by good essay questions than the sheer ability to remember and reproduce information. There has been a rather large-scale movement in colleges across the United States in recent years to encourage critical-thinking skills. And it is believed that one of the primary ways this is done is by requesting students to write reflectively, thoughtfully, and analytically about the subject matter that they are learning. So you can expect, depending on the assumptions and attitudes of particular instructors, an increasing emphasis on essay examinations.

Earlier in this chapter I used the term *creative thinking*. Essay examinations can assess not only critical thinking but also creative thinking, which are not identical. (They do, of course, overlap.) Critical thinking is characterized by *logic*. Creative thinking, on the other hand, is characterized by *originality*. If your essay answer "jumps the rails" and develops ideas in new and unexpected directions, then it is creative. On the whole, you had better *not* do this unless you are *very sure* of what you are saying, why you are saying it, and where you are going with your ideas. The truth of the matter is that although instructors pay great lip service to the word *creativity*, they generally do not set up situations that either require or encourage it. Critical thinking, on the other hand, *is* encouraged and recognized.

In the vast majority of cases you can easily ascertain from the way an essay question is worded if the instructor is looking for any creativity in the answer. Here are some examples of essay questions from different disciplines that do in fact require critical thinking but do not require creativity:

1. Compare the writing styles and general approaches of Ernest Hemingway and Raymond Chandler.
2. What were some of the common causes of World War I and World War II?
3. How does the concept of free will differ from the concept of determinism?
4. Why do behavior therapists tend to make little use of Freud's concept of an unconscious mental life?

Here are some examples of essay questions that emphasize creative thinking:

1. Develop this proposition: In the year 2050 the United States will be blighted, overpopulated, and resemble one of today's underdeveloped countries.
2. Imagine that you are Herman Melville living today. What would be some of your observations about contemporary life?
3. Take the position that Socrates was not a man of courage after all. Show how he could be called a coward.
4. It is popular in abnormal psychology these days to say that infantile autism has a genetic basis. Try to present an opposed viewpoint.

These last four questions would dismay the vast majority of students, and rightly so. Not only do they require creative thinking, but they also require an even larger range of knowledge than do most essay questions. In order to think creatively in any worthwhile, substantive way about a subject, one must also have a solid foundation of information and supporting critical-thinking skills. Perhaps for this reason most instructors limit their writing requests to those that assess primarily critical thinking.

HOW TO ANALYZE QUESTIONS

Multiple-choice questions and essay questions require different kinds of analytical skills. First, let's explore those associated with multiple-choice questions.

A principal point to be made is this: "*Yes*, it is necessary to analyze a multiple-choice question." A common attitude among students is: "Read a multiple-choice question quickly, strike it a sort of glancing psychological blow, and go with your first impression. Don't change an answer. Your first reaction is almost certainly the right one."

I have had this attitude expressed to me in a variety of ways over the years. It is an incorrect attitude and is based on mistaken assumptions.

One mistaken assumption is that analysis and logic are not required to sort out correct and incorrect answers. Many students believe that the right answer is supposed to jump out instantly, stand out like a waving figure against a static background. The right answer will not necessarily stick out its hand and greet you with "Welcome, here I am." Often it is shy, and you have to seek it out. You do this by proceeding with caution, thinking about each answer, and invoking a process of elimination. The best multiple-choice questions are those that require this process, and this is the kind that the vast majority of instructors try to write. The idea is to present a set of answers that all have a superficial plausibility. Therefore, don't be discouraged if you have to do some mental work to dig out the best one out of four or five choices.

What about changing an answer that is already marked on your answer sheet? When you change an answer, you are obviously engaged in evaluative thought. You are in doubt, and you are demonstrating a behavior based on a logical analysis. Research suggests that if a student changes 10 or 12 answers in a 50-question test, about 30 percent of the changes will have an adverse impact on the overall score. Seventy percent will have a positive impact on the overall score. So there is a net gain. The obvious conclusion is: Read questions carefully and change answers if they seem to need changing. You are not flying blind, nor should you.

In the case of essay questions, the process of analysis should revolve around this self-posed question: "What learning does the instructor want me to demonstrate?" The instructor has tried to convey some concepts and certain connections between them. The essay question itself, no matter how it is posed, is an attempt to assess if the teacher's objectives have made the bridge to the mind of the student. Let's take one of the essay questions I presented earlier, and develop a strategy for analyzing it.

Question 1. Compare the writing styles and general approaches of Ernest Hemingway and Raymond Chandler. This question asks you in essence: "What are the similarities and differences between the writing styles and general approaches of these two authors?" An effective image to use is two large overlapping circles. If you like, you can actually draw the circles on a piece of scratch paper before you write your essay. Label the circles A and B. Let A stand for Ernest Hemingway and let B stand for

Raymond Chandler. The common overlapping area between the circles is called the set *intersect*. It is this that is the most important.

Make a list of traits that belong in circle A. Then make a list of traits that belong in circle B. Finally, make a list of all of the traits that belong in the set intersect. For example, in circle A, Hemingway's circle, your rough notes might say: (1) Wrote several novels with war as a setting—*A Farewell to Arms* and *For Whom the Bell Tolls*; (2) was considered a serious novelist; (3) wrote terse, to-the-point prose with few metaphors. In circle B, Chandler's circle, your rough notes might say: (1) Wrote detective novels—*The Big Sleep* and *The Long Goodbye*; (2) was not considered a serious novelist in his lifetime; and (3) wrote in the first person in a wordy, almost poetic way.

So far so good. But if differences between the authors are all you can think of, your instructor will not be impressed. The set intersect shows that you can *synthesize*, bring material together. So now make a list of *similarities* that you think you can defend. The self-posed question here is: "How are the writing styles and general approaches of Hemingway and Chandler alike?" Here are some similarities you might list: (1) Both Hemingway and Chandler dealt with heros in extreme, dangerous situations; (2) both used a lot of dialogue; and (3) both depended on overt action and violence to move the story along.

In the actual writing of the essay, elaborate with full sentences and examples on the traits you have identified. Start with the differences first. Write a paragraph or two on Hemingway's traits. Then write a paragraph or two on Chandler's traits. End by writing several paragraphs on their common traits.

You can apply this method of analysis, the overlapping circles, to almost any essay question you are asked. You will see that in most cases what the instructor is looking for is your ability to synthesize, to detect common elements, or similarities, among concepts. The approach I have presented not only helps you analyze essay questions, but also it suggests a plan of organization and writing that will stand you in good stead.

PRACTICAL TIPS

When you take any examination, be aware of the formal distinction made in Chapter 6 between learning itself and performance. *Learning* refers to what you actually know about a subject. *Performance* refers to your capacity to make that learning evident to others—in this case, to an instructor. The following practical tips are designed to enhance your performance. Consequently, they can help you pick up a few points, improve an examination score, and earn a higher grade.

Here are some tips associated with multiple-choice tests:

- Be sure you complete the test. Sometimes students leave a group of questions blank at the end of the test, having worked too slowly and too carefully on the first portion of the test. Most instructors do not penalize for guessing. Consequently, any answer is better than none. If each question has four choices, you will get one-fourth of the answers right by chance alone.

- Be sure you have answered every question. Go over the test and double-check. Students often skip over two or three questions and needlessly lose points.

- After you have completed the test, reevaluate stubborn questions and consider changing answers. This point has been made before: You are more likely to pick up overall points from a process of double-checking and making changes than by blindly trusting your first impressions.

- Many answer sheets these days are machine graded. Consequently it is essential that all marks be dark and in accordance with instructions. Usually marks are made with a Number 2 pencil. When you make a change, erase completely and thoroughly. An optical scanner will pick up stray marks and incomplete erasures, interpret these as two answers where only one is allowed, and mark a given item as wrong.

- Ask your instructor if you can use a standard dictionary. Often you will find that looking up a single word will make a previously obscure multiple-choice question into a clear one. This is not cheating because the examination is not over your general vocabulary. Most instructors will cooperate with a request to be allowed a dictionary.

- If English is a second language for you, ask the instructor if you can bring in an English–foreign language dictionary. Don't hesitate to ask. This request is quite appropriate, and most instructors will agree to it.

- Study for multiple-choice tests by the recall method. Such a method was described in detail in Chapter 5. Although a multiple-choice test is a recognition test, the general rule is this: *If you can recall an item, you can certainly recognize it.* Recognition is the easier of the two memory tasks, and it proceeds best on a foundation made up of the capacity to recall at will.

Here are some tips associated with essay examinations:

- Give your essay an organization. Don't just ramble and free associate. Decide what point or points you want to make and proceed to make them.

- Don't consciously strive for a literary style. The purpose of an essay examination is primarily evaluative. It is a test, a device for assessing learning. Consequently, you should say what you need to say as directly and as clearly as possible. Some students try to obscure a lack of knowledge with allegories, metaphors, and lengthy anecdotes. You won't fool the instructor.

- An essay question gives you the opportunity to demonstrate your grasp of basic information and your capacity for critical thinking about a given subject. Consequently, try to work into the essay all of the relevant, specific ideas or facts that you can muster. Use terms, names, and define concepts. Also, make connections between concepts. Tie ideas together. Demonstrate your capacity to detect similarities.

- Seek to make your essay an optimal length. An essay that is too short will seem to be a minimal, feeble effort. Three or four sentences is not an essay. An essay that is too long will seem to be padded. The instructor will perhaps think that you are overstuffing it just to give it bulk in a misguided effort to make it artificially impressive. Student essays that run over 1,000 words (about five to six handwritten pages) are usually too long. It is, of course, impossible to give you an ideal length for every essay because much depends on the nature of the questions asked, the number of questions asked, and so forth. Nonetheless, in my experience, the typical student essay runs in the vicinity of 400 to 500 words. This is about two or three handwritten pages and is the length of an average newspaper editorial.

- Make your essay as presentable as possible. Pay attention to spelling and grammar. And make your handwriting as clear and as legible as you can. Factors such as these have an impact on the grade the instructor assigns the essay.

CONCLUDING REMARKS

Remember that the art of taking examinations is just that, an *art*. An examination is an attempt to evaluate learning. As noted earlier, however, there is a formal distinction between learning itself and performance. Learning cannot be evaluated directly, but rather only through performance.

Consequently, you can pick up points on examinations, a highly desirable objective, by applying the kinds of insights and tips offered in this chapter.

It was noted in the introduction to this chapter that among students who are over 25, a frequently expressed idea is the notion that age in and of itself makes one a less competent test taker. Your age is no barrier to using the outlined strategies for taking exams. On the contrary, with maturity it is likely that you are less rash and impulsive than you were when you were younger. A calmer disposition allows you to settle down and take the time and trouble associated with making examination taking into an art.

KEY POINTS TO REMEMBER

- If you commonly experience test anxiety, you are not alone.
- Moderate anxiety has actually been found to facilitate test performance. Excessive and chronic anxiety is disruptive.
- A multiple-choice question challenges learning by invoking a memory retrieval process called *recognition.*
- Essay and short-answer fill-in-the-blank questions challenge learning by invoking a memory retrieval process called *recall.*
- From the instructional point of view, one of the main advantages of multiple-choice tests is that they allow for objective grading.
- If an absolute grading scale is too harsh, then an instructor may decide to grade on the curve.
- The primary purpose of an essay question is to assess your capacity to *tie together,* or *make connections* among, terms, concepts, and key pieces of information. In educational psychology this process is usually called *critical thinking.*
- Creative thinking, in contrast to critical thinking, is characterized by *originality.*
- It is necessary to analyze a multiple-choice question. The often-heard advice that one should not change already-marked answers is based on false assumptions.
- In the case of essay questions, the process of analysis should revolve around this self-posed question: "What learning does the instructor want me to demonstrate?"
- If an essay question asks you to make a comparison, use the overlapping circles method described in the chapter in order to make an analysis of similarities and differences.

- This chapter offered a number of practical tips for taking multiple-choice examinations, three of which are: (1) Be sure to complete the test, (2) reevaluate stubborn questions and consider changing answers, and (3) ask your instructor if you can use a standard dictionary.
- This chapter offered a number of practical tips for taking essay examinations, three of which are: (1) Organize your essay, (2) don't consciously strive for a literary style, and (3) seek to make your essay an optimal length.

13

COPING WITH LEARNED HELPLESSNESS

From Pessimism to Optimism

I recently asked students in a psychology class to complete the following sentence: "I feel helpless as a student when. . . . " I told them, "Names are not required on your papers. You don't have to write an essay. Just complete the sentence. And the first thing that pops into your mind is probably the best thing to put down."

Pens and pencils flew over the various sheets of paper. Over forty students were present, and most seemed to know what I meant by the phrase "feel helpless." Within ten minutes I had collected a batch of papers. All but two or three students knew immediately how they wanted to respond.

Here are seven of the answers I received:

"I feel helpless as a student when the jobs I want are out there but my degree is still so far away."

"I feel helpless as a student when I feel I'm not achieving anything and I start hating school."

"I feel helpless as a student when I'm at home doing homework or studying and don't really understand the subject."

"I feel helpless as a student when I cannot determine what an instructor expects from me when answering essay questions."

"I feel helpless as a student when I do not get enough time to study my subject."

"I feel helpless as a student when I don't understand what to study for."

"I feel helpless as a student when it comes to midterms and finals."

It is obvious that a feeling of helplessness is common. In some students it is brief, coming and going in a short time. In the case of other students the feeling of helplessness is chronic. It is a slow poison eroding both their self-confidence and the belief that they can achieve their academic goals. These students are in danger of dropping out of college, never to return. In the case of *all* students, a feeling of helplessness is corrosive and destructive.

If you are an adult with a burden of responsibilities such as the demands associated with a partner, children, a job, and bills to pay, these factors will aggravate and intensify the negative aspects of learned helplessness.

THE NATURE OF LEARNED HELPLESSNESS

A feeling of helplessness is just that, a *feeling*. It is not necessarily a reflection of objective reality. It frequently is the result of a self-defeating attitude, a way of looking at challenges and obstacles in terms of negative past experiences.

Psychologists make a formal distinction between actual helplessness and learned helplessness. *Actual helplessness* arises from a situation in which there is little or no way that you can control eventual outcomes. Examples include jumping into a cold ocean from the deck of a sinking ship, falling through the sky after both your main and secondary parachutes have failed to open, finding out that you have an inoperable and incurable cancer, and being held hostage. Although such situations can and do arise, they are far less common than situations in which you do have some element of control over outcomes.

Learned helplessness is an incorrect belief that one is powerless; it can have no effect on eventual outcomes. This kind of helplessness is a psychological generalization, a tendency to perceive situation B, a situation *now*, as similar to situation A, a situation *then*. There was failure or defeat in situation A. And the mind expects failure or defeat in situation B.

In order to obtain a clear picture of exactly how learned helplessness works it is instructive to take a look at a typical experiment using rats as subjects. Sixty rats are randomly assigned to two groups, thirty to a group. One group is designated the Control Group and another group is designated the Experimental Group. In all of the experimental events to be described, the rats are tested one at a time. Members of the Control Group are placed in a conditioning apparatus designed to train rats to escape from a painful electrical shock. With repeated trials, each rat learns the appropriate escape behavior.

Members of the Experimental Group are placed in the same apparatus. However, they are subjected to *inescapable shock*. A transparent barrier prevents them from jumping off of a shock grid onto a safe zone. With repeated trials, each rat, because it is actually helpless, cringes and withdraws when it is shocked. It fails to make additional efforts to escape. This is the *training phase* of the experiment.

The next phase is the *test phase* of the experiment. Members of the Control Group are placed in a tank of deep water with high sides. The only thing to do if there is any possibility of survival is to swim. Rats are good swimmers. Each rat in the Control Group swims for an average of three hours, at which point the rat is exhausted and will have to be rescued if it is to avoid drowning. When members of the Experimental Group are placed in the tank, each rat in the group swims for an average of only a few minutes. At this point they must be rescued to save them from drowning.

If these were human beings, we would say that the subjects in the Control Group displayed heroic efforts, will, courage, and a refusal to accept defeat until there was no option left. Subjects in the Experimental Group displayed a lack of will and courage. They accepted defeat almost immediately. It is, of course, the subjects in the Experimental Group that suffer from learned helplessness. Because the rats were randomly assigned to the two conditions it seems evident that the differences in swimming behavior cannot be assigned to individual differences in the rats but to their *learning history*.

Assuming that the basic process of learned helplessness is roughly similar in rats and human beings, it is now easy to understand the basic nature of the phenomenon. It is a *generalization*. The organism, rat or human being, perceives a similarity between the past and the present. An error of perception is made. The organism says through its behavior that the present situation *is*, for all intents and purposes, the past situation. As you can see, learned helplessness is an insidious phenomenon that invades our lives in a highly adverse way.

HOW LEARNED HELPLESSNESS UNDERMINES ACADEMIC PERFORMANCE

The student who has a "bad" case of learned helplessness is defeated before he or she even starts. Like a rat in the Experimental Group, a few feeble efforts may be made and then the individual gives up. For example, Dwight J., 28, is married and the father of three children. He works full time in the produce department of a supermarket. He has a good job with benefits, but he dislikes his work with a passion. He grumbles and gripes all of the time about how he has no future, how he's stuck in a dead-end job, how handling produce is wet, cold work, and so forth. His wife, who sees a lot of intelligence and blocked potential in Dwight, encourages him to take evening classes at a local community college. Dwight, who dropped out of high school when he was 17, received grades in the tenth and eleventh grades that were mostly Ds and Fs with a smattering of Cs. He was raised in a single-parent household with four other children by a mother who abused alcohol. It is quite probable that Dwight's poor academic record in high school was due *not* to a lack of basic intelligence or ability but arose from an unsettled emotional state when he was an adolescent. Be that as it may, Dwight experienced too many academic defeats in high school, and he now has an extremely poor self-image as a student.

After repeated urgings from his wife, Dwight signs up for an evening class in beginning drafting at a local community college. He likes to draw and sketch, and he has a talent for making detailed copies of pictures of machines, diagrams, and house plans published in magazines. Before Dwight's first class there is much happy chatter between he and his wife about how he can become a draftsman by taking night classes, then work for an architect, and maybe someday become an architect himself. But they both know that the conversation has a hollow ring. A false optimism is being applied, like make-up, over the face of learned helplessness.

On the night of the first class, the instructor, a man with an authoritarian personality, sets forth his rules. He tells the group that he expects assignments to be done on time, that only two absences are allowed for sickness or emergencies all semester, that an expensive textbook must be purchased and studied carefully for tests, and so forth.

Dwight is discouraged. Nonetheless, he makes himself return for a second class. But the imposing demeanor of the instructor, the information-rich textbook, and the demands of the first assignment intimidate him. He doesn't do the assignment and he does not go to the third class. He never returns. He has decided he can't do college work, and he can't. However, the reason he can't do college work is because of learned helplessness. He really believes that he is ineffective and incompetent, and this attitude becomes a self-fulfilling prophecy.

Most students don't have a case of learned helplessness that is as severe as Dwight's. Nonetheless, elements of learned helplessness, specific in nature, often undermine academic performance. Many students have an attitude of learned helplessness—as was revealed in the group of student answers presented at the beginning of the chapter—toward examinations, writing assignments, oral presentations, English classes, math classes, science classes, lectures, haughty instructors, and textbooks. In short, almost anything and everything that challenges the individual in college can induce a degree of learned helplessness in a given student. When learned helplessness is induced, the student makes either no effort at all or only a feeble effort. Then the student drops a class, doesn't turn in a required assignment, or otherwise finds a way to avoid the challenge. And this behavior, of course, leads to poor grades and defeat.

COPING STRATEGIES

When you begin to feel helpless as a result of a task or challenge arising from academic demands, apply one or several of the following coping strategies.

- Ask yourself, "Am I actually helpless in this situation? Or is this a case of *feeling* helpless because of learned helplessness?" Use this question to make an appraisal. You will find that in most situations you are not *completely* helpless, and there is much you can do to help yourself. Turn to the specific advice given in other chapters of this book, advice designed to help you be an effective student.

- Be aware that although learned helplessness is a phenomenon that affects both rats and human beings you have something the rat doesn't have. You have the power to *reflect* on your own behavior. You can think about thinking. This is something the rat cannot do. By the process of rational thought and reflection it is possible to break out of the negative emotional state induced by learned helplessness. This chapter and the coping strategies offered are designed to make you more self-aware. And self-awareness is the key to breaking self-defeating emotional habits such as learned helplessness.

- Focus on internal locus of control, not external locus of control. When a person tends to focus on *internal locus of control*, he or she feels in charge of life. Behavior is perceived as arising from *within* oneself. Its source, or locus, appears to be one's own intelligence and will. On the other hand, when a person tends to focus on *external locus of control*, he or she feels like a victim, a pawn of fate. Behavior is perceived as arising from *outside* oneself. Its source, or locus, appears to be other people, adverse circumstances, lack of opportunity, the rotten "System," stupid course requirements, and so forth. It is important that you say something like this to yourself: "I refuse to play the role of the victim. I am *not* a pawn of fate. I have will and intelligence and I place myself at the helm of my own destiny!"

- Remember that learned helpless is just that, *learned*. What can be learned can be unlearned. Learned helpless should be thought of as a pathological, useless habit. It can be broken, or modified, like any other habit.

- Adopt the point of view that the idea that you are helpless in certain academic situations is a *psychological* construct, a view of reality. Once you realize that your psychological world is *built by you*— "constructed"—you can separate this world from the real, objective world and gain greater control over your own behavior.

LEARNED OPTIMISM

Martin Seligman, the researcher who introduced the concept of learned helplessness into the psychological literature, has recently developed a concept called *learned optimism*. Just as it is possible to generalize negative experiences from the past to the present, so it is also possible to generalize *positive* experiences from the past to the present. One can assert, for example, that the rats in the Control Group, willing to swim to the point of exhaustion, manifested learned optimism. They had a history of success; they were *effective* in escaping from shock. Consequently, in a new situation, they displayed energy and persistence.

A rat must depend on its learning history for states of learned helplessness or learned optimism. This is probably true of all organisms except human beings. Birds, dogs, and horses cannot stand back from their own experiences and undo the adverse effects of the past. However, as I have indicated earlier, human beings seem to have the power not only to think, but also to *think about thinking*. It appears that this power can be used, as indicated by the coping strategies, to develop a state of learned optimism. And this is true *regardless of your past experiences*.

Work toward developing learned optimism. When you are presented with an academic challenge in the form of an examination, an assignment, an essay, a term paper, or an oral report, use learned optimism to rise to the challenge.

CONCLUDING REMARKS

Age is no barrier to the acquisition of learned optimism. On the contrary, it seems reasonable to suggest that with maturity you become *more* capable of reflection and self-analysis, *more* capable of freeing yourself from the adverse effects of defeats in your own life history. Say to yourself, and mean it: "It's never too late."

KEY POINTS TO REMEMBER

- A feeling of helplessness is common in students.
- *Actual helplessness* arises from a situation in which there is little or no way that one can control eventual outcomes.
- *Learned helplessness* is an incorrect belief that one is powerless and can have no effect on eventual outcomes.
- An individual's *learning history* is what resides behind a self-defeating feeling of helplessness.
- Learned helplessness is a *generalization* from the past to the present. The organism says through its behavior that the present situation *is*, for all intents and purposes, the past situation.

- The student who has a "bad" case of learned helplessness is defeated before he or she even starts.
- Elements of learned helplessness, specific in nature, often undermine academic performance.
- Ask yourself, "Am I actually helpless in this situation?"
- You can think about thinking, something that other organisms probably cannot do. And this ability can help you to free yourself from learned helplessness.
- Focus on internal locus of control, not external locus of control.
- Remember that learned helplessness is just that, *learned*. What can be learned can be unlearned.
- Adopt the point of view that the idea that you are helpless in certain academic situations is a *psychological construct*, a view of reality.
- The concept of *learned optimism* asserts that it is possible to generalize *positive* experiences from the past to the present.
- Age is no barrier to the acquisition of learned optimism. Adopt the attitude that it's never too late.

| 4

DEVELOPING AN OUTSTANDING MEMORY

Tricks of the Trade

Most of us believe, and believe correctly, that a good memory is an important factor in academic success.

But what is a "good" memory?

Is it inborn?

Can it be acquired?

If it can be acquired, how can you develop an outstanding one?

And how does age affect memory?

These questions will be addressed in this chapter.

THE CLASSICAL, OUTDATED VIEW OF MEMORY

Ancient philosophers thought of memory as a *mental faculty*, a power of the mind. This faculty was primarily inborn. It was naturally weak in some people and naturally strong in others. This view held sway well into the early part of the twentieth century, and it still persists today. It is "common sense" to believe that some of us are blessed with better memory abilities than others. This venerable belief is reinforced by clinical reports of mentally disabled *savants*, people who often have unusual memory abilities. A *savant* is a "wise" person, and the word *savvy* refers to traits such as comprehension and understanding. The motion picture *Rain Man*, in which Dustin Hoffman played a savant and Tom Cruise his brother, is an entertaining presentation of an individual with not only a remarkable memory but also other interesting mental abilities.

However, the existence of savants, as interesting as they and their abilities are, does not have much to do with the general idea that ordinary people have great individual differences in their memory abilities. Research on human learning suggests that the vast majority of people have "good" memories, meaning their memories function quite well if certain effective strategies are employed.

Contemporary learning theorists tend to believe that the classical view of memory as an inborn power, as a sort of psychological "thing" in the mind, is outdated. The very word *memory* is a noun, and you were taught somewhere along the line that a noun is a person, place, or thing. Well, memory is neither a person nor a place, so, by default it must be a thing. But, of course, it is *not* a thing.

What *is* it then? It is a *process*, a way in which information is dealt with by the mind. It is this view, the modern one, that we will employ in this chapter. And, armed with this view, it will be possible to see how you can greatly improve your memory abilities.

HOW MEMORY WORKS

Memory is a process involving the encoding, storage, and retrieval of mental information. *Encoding* is a subprocess characterized by the conversion of raw sensory information into a form that makes it easier to store and retrieve. What adults see and hear is, by and large, automatically converted into numerals, words, and other symbols. These in turn become parts of larger patterns such as mathematical equations and sentences. On the whole, we think and remember in terms of symbols that represent external reality. And these symbols—characteristic of mathematics and language—constitute a process of encoding.

In view of the fact that the activity of encoding is the first step in the memory process, it is the target of most of the memory strategies designed to improve memory functioning. Examples of this will be given later under the heading, "Mnemonic Devices or Memory Strategies."

Storage is a subprocess in which the encoded versions of events and ideas (i.e., "memories") are put away for future use. Where are they "put"? Again, the commonsense notion of memory as a kind of thing comes into play. Memories are put in the "memory bank" just as cash is put in the money bank. Both reflection and research suggest, however, that memories are not stored like physical objects. Storage, as suggested above, is a *subprocess* of memory. Something is happening. Memory storage consists of a series of ongoing mental events.

At the neurological level, storage appears to take place because of two related factors. The first factor is changes in RNA (ribonucleic acid) molecules in neurons. *Neurons* are living cells in the brain and nervous system that specialize in the transmission of information. Experiences and events appear to change the structure of RNA molecules. These changes in turn affect the way in which a neuron manufactures *neurotransmitters*, chemical messengers that make communication between neurons possible. Certain neurotransmitters appear to be of more importance than others in the case of memory.

The second factor is changes in the way in which neurons form themselves into groups. Experiences appear to affect neuron organization in such a way that they tend to shape themselves into circuits of cells. Donald O. Hebb, a pioneer researcher into the nature of mental organization, called these circuits *cell assemblies*, which appear to be the neurological analogues of recorded experience. Think of them as the basic building blocks of memory, but also keep in mind that cell assemblies are *alive*. They can grow and change. And, also, they can decay and disorganize themselves. At the behavioral level, we tend to use words such as *learning* and *remembering* for positive changes. Words such as *forgetting* and phrases such as "My memory is playing tricks on me" suggest negative changes.

A discussion of biological processes involved in memory may seem rather remote from personal experience. However, it has practical applications, as you will see in the next section, "The Health of Your Brain."

This is the logical place to answer one of the questions posed at the beginning of this chapter: "How does age affect memory?" The general answer, with qualifications, is: "Very little." If you are anywhere between 20 and 70, and you are in good health, age will not, in and of itself, have a heavy adverse impact on memory. Studies using standardized intelligence tests such as the Wechsler Adult Intelligence Scale (WAIS) suggest that a decline in functional memory of no more than 2 to 5 percent can be expected over a range of many years. Even people who are in their seventies and eighties often have almost unimpaired memory abilities. The important point for you to realize is that it is highly unlikely that you have any memory impairment due to your age.

The above statements do not, of course, apply to persons who suffer from an organic condition that impairs memory. Alzheimer's disease is one example of such a condition. There will be more about organic aspects of memory in the next section, in which the health of the brain is discussed.

Retrieval is a subprocess that allows us to recover stored information and bring it back to a conscious level. There are two basic modes of retrieval—recall and recognition. *Recall* involves the voluntary retrieval of information with a minimum of sensory assistance. For example, you look at a person's face and try to recall the name that goes with it. There is nothing to assist you, you don't have a set of likely names in front of you, and there are no initials in evidence, so the burden is completely on your capacity to recall. Recall is the most demanding kind of retrieval. It is the mode demanded by an essay examination or a short-answer fill-in-the-blank test. Recall is fairly easy when information has been well learned, but it is next to impossible when information has been barely learned.

Recognition involves the selection of a correct piece of information from an array of both correct and incorrect items. Here there is a maximum of sensory assistance, and the burden on the retrieval process is fairly light. Let's say you cannot recall a person's name. You are told it is one of four names: Bill, Frank, Jim, or Harry. And you say, easily and correctly, "Of course. It's Jim." Recognition is the mode demanded by true-false and multiple-choice questions. It is possible to make accurate recognitions even when information has been barely learned.

The familiar *tip-of-the-tongue phenomenon* is associated with the recall subprocess. You are likely to say that a name or other item is on the tip of your tongue when it is barely learned and you can almost, but not quite, recall it. The information is stored, but you can't retrieve it.

Two very important psychological processes interfere with effective retrieval. These are repression and forgetting. *Repression* is an active process. The ego defends itself against forbidden wishes and painful childhood memories by banishing such information to an unconscious level of the mind. Repressed information cannot be retrieved by a normal act of voluntary recall. Retrieval requires special methods such as hypnosis or free association in a psychoanalytic session.

Forgetting, in commonsense terms, is a "weakening" or a "fading" of memories. The popular view is that old memories are like old photographs, dull and indistinct. This view of memory, while serviceable enough for everyday life, is probably an overly simple one. Research on memory suggests that forgetting, like repression, is an active process. New information "rewrites" old memories. There are systematic distortions. And, often, very old memories from one's childhood and adolescence are particularly vivid—even though the events associated with them took place long ago.

A substantial amount of forgetting can take place in a relatively short time. That is why it is important to review and refresh one's memory of key points shortly before an examination.

THE HEALTH OF YOUR BRAIN

It is impossible to have an effectively functioning memory without a healthy brain. As already indicated, memory depends totally upon *neurons*, living cells in the brain and nervous system. It is estimated that you have about 3 billion neurons in your brain, whereas the population of the United States is 250 million. So you have twelve times as many neurons in your brain as there are people in this country. That's a lot of neurons!

You don't acquire neurons with age. And they can't regenerate themselves once they die. You have all of the neurons you are ever going to have when you are an infant. Consequently, it is greatly to your advantage to nurture them and to protect them. They are, without question, one of the greatest assets you have. This section suggest ways you can give your neurons the TLC, or tender loving care, they deserve.

Good Nutrition

Neurons, like all cells of the body, thrive on a balanced diet. Children in underdeveloped countries who grow up on less than 14 percent protein frequently suffer from mental retardation associated with lack of proper maturation of the brain and nervous system. What is true in childhood is to some extent also true in adulthood. To exaggerate, if you were to eat a diet made up primarily of carbohydrates, complex or refined, such as bread, potatoes, pancakes, cookies, pie, soft drinks, and candy, your neurons would struggle to survive. You also need some milk, eggs, cheese, chicken, beef, and fish.

Lack of protein is seldom a problem in the United States, where most adults get about 30 percent protein in their diets. Nonetheless, lack of protein can be a problem if you focus on carbohydrate foods and avoid proteins. Also, if you are a vegetarian, you need to know what you are doing. For example, if you eat beans and bread at the same meal, you will get a complete protein source with all of the amino acids. If you eat beans only, or bread only, at a given meal, you will be slighting yourself in terms of protein. Protein is of such paramount importance because it is the basic building block of *protoplasm*, the stuff from which your cells are made.

In connection with adequate supplies of proteins you need adequate supplies of the micronutrients called vitamins. The word *vitamin* evolved from an older term, *vital amines*. Vitamins, or vital amines, are organic compounds that facilitate biochemical processes. They play an important role in the case of memory because they are utilized, and used up, in the manufacture by neurons of neurotransmitters, the chemical messengers that make communication between neurons—and therefore memory—possible.

The B-complex vitamins are of particular importance in the manufacture of key neurotransmitters. These vitamins are really a family consisting of 11 related vitamins such as thiamine, riboflavin, and folic acid. It is beyond the scope of this book to present a complete list of food sources for the B-complex vitamins, but good sources include wheat germ, milk, various meats, whole-wheat bread, various fruits, peanuts, and leafy green vegetables.

If you eat on the run and don't eat balanced meals, as many students do, it is probably a good idea to take a daily multiple-vitamin capsule as a nutritional supplement. Such a capsule contains not only B-complex vitamins, but other vitamins as well as important minerals.

Aerobic Exercise

Neurons thrive on oxygen. Deprived of oxygen, they die. Consequently, cardiovascular fitness will assure you of a steady supply of oxygen to your neurons. In order to attain, or maintain, cardiovascular fitness it is important to obtain a certain amount of aerobic exercise. *Aerobic exercise* is exercise that places a little extra demand on your heart. You can tell when activity is aerobic because your respirations increase and your pulse becomes more rapid.

The student's life is a sedentary one. Perhaps you protest. "I'm a busy parent as well as a student. I have a part-time job too. I'm on the run all day. I get plenty of exercise." Unfortunately, it is not true that being busy and active all day gives you plenty of exercise. The exercise is not, as indicated above, aerobic. You never get your heart rate to a sufficiently rapid rate for a sustained period of time.

The ideal way to obtain aerobic exercise is with the aid of a pulse meter. Various books and charts suggest that an exercise, or training, pulse rate ranging between 165 to 135 beats per minute is optimal for persons between 20 and 29 years of age. The optimal range goes down with age. Between 30 and 39 it is between 160 and 130 beats per minute. When you reach 60, the optimal range is between 140 and 110 beats per minute. The training pulse should be sustained for 20 to 30 minutes three or four times per week.

If you cannot seem to adapt to a systematic exercise program, then a simple and basic recommendation is to take a brisk walk at least three times per week. The word "brisk" suggests a fast, but comfortable, pace. The walk should be sustained, without a break, for about twenty minutes. A mild, comfortable program such as this one will give you much of the benefit of a more systematic aerobic program.

If you have doubts about your health or are out of condition, be sure you consult a physician before you embark on *any* exercise program.

As indicated above, your neurons need oxygen, because they will suffer and function poorly if deprived of it. It is important, if you are to have an effectively functioning memory, to pay some attention to cardiovascular fitness.

Avoiding Refined Carbohydrates

A diet that is too high in refined carbohydrates tends to induce at first a brief high sugar state, or *hyperglycemia*. Then there is a rebound effect, and there follows a longer low blood sugar state, or *hypoglycemia*. This variation in blood sugars is mild in younger persons in good health because of the body's self-adjusting mechanisms. In somewhat older persons the tendency toward hypoglycemia may be more pronounced, and some individuals are much more prone to hypoglycemia than others.

Refined carbohydrates are foods loaded with sugar and white flour. Readily digested foods such as potatoes and white rice are not, strictly speaking, refined carbohydrates, but they function in the body almost as if they were. Examples of foods high in refined carbohydrates are cakes, pies, doughnuts, candy bars, pancakes, waffles, jelly sandwiches made with white bread, ice cream, and cookies. Beverages made with a lot of sugar, such as soft drinks and iced tea, can also be included in the refined carbohydrate category.

When you are in a low-blood-sugar state you feel sluggish. Your brain doesn't work right because your neurons are not supplied with an optimal amount of blood sugar in the form of glucose. Arousal and ability to concentrate are both adversely affected. There is no way your memory can work best under these conditions.

Also, the biochemical processes associated with refined carbohydrates use up B-complex vitamins. Consequently, the B-complex vitamins available for the manufacture of neurotransmitters involved in memory are depleted. As indicated earlier, a low level of B-complex vitamins tends to have an adverse impact on memory. Consequently, all logic suggests that in order to have an effectively functioning memory it is important to avoid refined carbohydrates.

Alcohol Consumption

The consumption of alcohol has a negative impact on the health of the brain's neurons. Persons who abuse alcohol for a prolonged period of time sometimes suffer from *alcohol amnestic disorder*, also known as *Korsakoff's psychosis*. One of the principal symptoms of the disorder is memory impairment. The disorder is caused by damage to the central nervous system due to a low level of *thiamine*, a B-complex vitamin.

It is doubtful that moderate drinking has an adverse impact on the brain. Nonetheless, alcohol is a drug, and the very existence of alcohol amnestic disorder suggests that it is a drug that is not good for the brain. Consequently, it is important to make a distinction between alcohol *use* and alcohol *abuse*. One has to steer clearly away from abuse if one's neurons, and one's memory, are to work as they should.

MNEMONIC DEVICES OR MEMORY STRATEGIES

This section offers you specific skills and techniques that will improve the way in which your memory functions. The discussion that follows goes under the general heading of *metamemory*, memory "above" or "beyond" memory itself. Metamemory implies not only remembering, but also *remembering to remember*. If you remember to use the techniques to be outlined, you will have a better day-to-day working memory.

A *mnemonic device* is an aid to memory, something that gives memory a boost. The word *mnemonic* comes from a Greek root meaning, simply, memory. The familiar word *amnesia* is a first cousin to *mnemonic*. The first letter, *a*, means "without." The rest of the word, *mnesia*, refers to memory. Thus *amnesia* means "without memory." The art of using mnemonic devices is called *mnemonics*. Mnemonic devices are the tricks of the memory trade, and they are often used by professional entertainers who demonstrate unusual memory abilities.

Although the terms *mnemonic device* and *mnemonics* are the more traditional terms, it might be better to speak of memory strategies. The older terms imply "gimmicks"—cute and clever ways of remembering. Although these certainly have a place, they are only one kind of tool in your memory kit. Let's explore the principal memory strategies and how to apply them to your own advantage.

Understanding Concepts

It is common to hear people say, "You will forget most of what you learn in college." This is somewhat true about facts and details, but it is not true of concepts. Concept learning, the most important learning that takes place in higher education, requires insight and understanding. (See "The Advantages of Insight Learning" in Chapter 6.) When you learn a concept you learn an *idea*.

In many modern textbooks the key concepts for the subject under study can be found in a marginal glossary. (If not, there is almost always an alphabetical glossary toward the end of the book.) The definition represents a summary statement of the concept, and the term is a tag or hook that provides the mind with access to the concept.

It is not necessary that you memorize definitions word for word, but it *is* necessary that you get the general idea, or, in other words, obtain an insight. Having said this, it is not harmful to memorize a definition *if* you do in fact understand the concept.

Let's say that you are taking an astronomy class and learn that a *light year* is the distance that light can travel in space in one year. "Light year" is the term. "The distance that light can travel in space in one year" is the definition. If you understand the definition, you have grasped the concept. Let's say you also learn that the speed of light is seven miles per second, and that the total distance of a light year is approximately 6,000,000,000,000 (6 trillion) miles. Ten years after you graduate from college someone asks you, "What's the speed of light?" Perhaps you have forgotten the *exact* speed, but you know it's "very fast." If you are asked for the distance involved in a light year, perhaps you have forgotten the numbers themselves, but you know it is a "long, long way." However, say that you are asked, "What is a light year?" Now you know the answer. "It's the distance that light can travel in a year." You *have* retained the basic concept, the most important thing. You can easily look up the exact numbers.

Your first and most important memory strategy is to focus on concepts. Information learned with insight is remembered for years and years. In fact, it's almost impossible to forget it.

Making a Picture

It has been wisely said that "A picture is worth a thousand words." We are much more likely to remember pictures than sentences. Consequently, whenever possible, try to turn ideas and facts into pictures. These pictures can be rough cartoons or outline drawings on paper. Or they can be mental pictures.

In the above definition of a light year, it is helpful to see two suns in the mind's eye. Visualize a beam of light traveling from one sun to the next sun. If the beam takes four years to get from Sun 1 to Sun 2, they are four light years apart. This mental picture can, of course, be made into a crude cartoon on a piece of paper. Light can be represented as a long arrow going from Sun 1 to Sun 2. Once this is done, your grasp of the concept of a light year is likely to be strongly reinforced.

When I teach Freud's theory of personality I say, "Freud said that the personality has three parts, the id, the ego, and the superego. Some people say that this is the house that Freud built." Then I make on the blackboard a cartoon drawing of a house, the kind almost any preschooler can make. The drawing consists of a foundation, the house proper, and the roof. The foundation is labeled "the id." The house proper is labeled "the ego." And the roof is labeled "the superego." Naturally, there is elaboration and discussion of the concepts. However, this simple drawing tends to be remembered, and it helps students comprehend how the three parts of the personality relate to each other.

Let's say that you are taking a course in statistics. You are told that the standard deviation is a measure of dispersion. In order to visualize dispersion, make a drawing of two targets. Dots or little x's on the targets represent hits, or scores. Target A is drawn with most of the hits near the bull's-eye. Target B is drawn with hits all over it. The scores on Target B display more dispersion than the scores on Target A. By making the drawings of the two targets you have turned an abstract concept into a concrete one. And in turn you have provided a way in which your memory can work efficiently.

General Facts—Lists, Names, and Dates

The least important kind of learning that takes place in college is made up of general information. This consists of facts—lists, names, and dates. Nonetheless, whether you can remember general information long enough to recall or recognize it on an examination will have a profound effect upon your grades. Consequently, you need a way make your memory work effectively when it is presented with general information.

The problem is that often general information is not meaningful in and of itself. It has no *intrinsic*, built-in meaning. It is often random in nature. It is for this kind of information that the mnemonic devices, those artificial structures that augment memory capacity, are most useful.

Let's say that you are taking a geography class and you are asked to learn the names of the five great lakes. A well-known mnemonic device associated with this task is the word *homes*. Each letter of the word is used to recall one of the lakes: H = Huron, O = Ontario, M = Michigan, E = Erie, and S = Superior.

What you need to do is make up your own mnemonic devices for specific general information that you are asked to learn. For example, let's say that you are taking an introductory psychology class and you are told that the founders of the five classical schools of psychology were Wundt, Wertheimer, Watson, James, and Freud. How can you make a mnemonic device out of this? One way is to look for patterns. Note that three of the names begin with a W. W's look something like valleys, so visualize the three W's as three valleys. Now make up a variation on the familiar nursery rhyme that begins, "Jack and Jill went up a hill to fetch a pail of water. . . . " For the names that begin with a J and an F, think of Jack, all alone without Jill, carrying a *full* pail of water. Now convert the whole image into a sentence and underline key words: *Jack*, carrying a *full* pail of water, fell down *three valleys*. Visualize Jack spilling a full pail of water as he rolls down three valleys, shaped like W's, on his way home. On the examination, you think of the sentence and your mental picture. And you easily recall that the five key personalities are Wundt, Wertheimer, Watson, James, and Freud by association with the key stimulus letters: W, W, W, J, and F.

I know that the above mnemonic device seems ridiculous and overworked. That is part of the point. You often have to stretch your imagination a little to come up with a device. Sometimes the devices don't seem very good. However, the time and energy invested in creating a device has a tendency to make it be remembered. And it can in turn help you remember what you need to remember for an examination.

The device described above is not the only one you might have created in order to remember the five founders of the classical schools. You could have also made up a sentence that worked in each stimulus letter. Here is an example, with the key letters underlined: "When will winter joyfully flee?" Recall the sentence when you are taking the examination, and you will have an effective way to recall the five key names. There are many devices you can make up for almost any general information you are required to learn.

There are two keys to remembering names for examinations. First, the name itself must be remembered. Second, the name must be connected, or associated, with a fact or concept. You can construct a single mnemonic device that will accomplish both results. For example, let's say that in a psychology class you want to remember that Abraham Maslow, a principal founder of humanistic psychology, believed that it was important for people to have *peak experiences*, brief moments of joy and ecstasy. Think of an Abraham you are already familiar with—Abraham Lincoln. If there is a picture of Maslow in your textbook, visualize him with a top hat and a beard. If not, just visualize Lincoln himself. Now in your mind's eye, using the figure you have picked, visualize him climbing to the top of a mountain and being ecstatic over the experience. The mountain top is the "peak." These combined images will make it possible for you to recall or recognize easily almost any association having to do with Abraham Maslow and peak experiences.

If you can't remember the last name, in this case, Maslow, convert it into concrete images—"things" or "objects." A sack of potatoes is a heavy "mass." Imagine that it is sitting on the ground, therefore it is "low." Imagine the Abraham figure with a top hat picking up the "mass" of potatoes from the "low" ground—and you have "Maslow." I am perfectly aware that all of this sounds rather silly, but, believe me, if you use your creative imagination in the way described, it *will* help you remember. Just try it. Let that be the proof of the pudding.

One easy way to remember a date is to relate the date to yourself. Let's say that in a history class you want to remember that the armistice for World War I was signed in 1918. Let's say that you were born in 1960. Subtract 1918 from 1960, and the answer is 42. Now say to yourself, "World War I ended 42 years before I was born—almost a half century before I was an infant." This is more meaningful than a random date. In order to remember the *exact* date, say to yourself, "Well, I know that it ended *this* century—so it has to begin with a 19." Now think of something you did that was particularly pleasant when you were 18—perhaps a date, a kiss, a memorable outing. Link this in your mind with the 19 and the phrase "the end of World War I." Now you have 19 + 18 or 1918.

Again, I know that all of this sounds overly involved, but that's because it takes time to explain it. In actual practice, the whole process is relatively rapid. The excess information, and the meaning, you add to the date helps you to remember it.

The basic principle running through all of the mnemonic devices used to remember general information such as lists, names, and dates is *similarity*. This was identified as a basic law of association in Chapter 6. Quoting from that chapter, the law of similarity says we tend to learn a new stimulus fairly readily if it is somewhat like an already learned stimulus.

When you use a mnemonic device, you take advantage of something you already know, or remember, and link it to something new, something to be remembered.

Creative, novel, vivid images make mnemonic devices work.

And, remember, you can enhance their effectiveness by converting them into rough cartoons.

CONCLUDING REMARKS

Two self-defeating ideas are held by many students. The first idea is, "I have a bad memory," and the second is, "My memory is going downhill because of my age." I have tried to show you in this chapter that both of these ideas are false.

Very few healthy students have a "bad" memory because it is defective in some way like an injured heart muscle or weak kidneys. Remember, the memory is *not* a thing. It is a process. You can make a "bad" memory into a good one by using your memory effectively, by taking advantage of the suggestions offered in this chapter.

Your age, as an independent causal factor, has almost no relevance to your functioning memory. Let's make two assumptions: Your health is good, and you know how to use your memory. Under these circumstances, over a wide range of years spanning many decades, you can expect to have a fully functioning memory.

KEY POINTS TO REMEMBER

- Ancient philosophers thought of memory as a *mental faculty*, a power of the mind.
- Contemporary psychologists focus on the importance of memory as a *process*, the way in which information is dealt with by the mind.
- *Memory* is a process involving the encoding, storage, and retrieval of mental information.
- *Encoding* is a subprocess characterized by the conversion of raw sensory information into a form that makes it easier to store and retrieve.
- *Storage* is a subprocess in which the encoded versions of events and ideas (i.e., "memories") are put away for future use.
- *Retrieval* is a subprocess that allows us to recover stored information and bring it back to a conscious level.

- *Recall* involves the voluntary retrieval of information with a minimum of sensory assistance.
- *Recognition* involves the selection of a correct piece of information from an array of both correct and incorrect items.
- *Neurons* are living cells in the brain and nervous system that specialize in the transmission of information.
- Good nutrition is important to the health of the brain.
- Aerobic exercise helps neurons thrive.
- A state of low blood sugar, or *hypoglycemia*, interferes with the action of neurons, and, in turn, the functioning of one's memory.
- Alcohol abuse has an adverse impact on the health of the brain's neurons, and, in turn, the functioning of one's memory.
- *Metamemory* is memory "above" or "beyond" memory itself. Metamemory implies not only remembering but also *remembering to remember.*
- A *mnemonic device* is an aid to memory, something that gives memory a boost.
- The best way to remember a concept is to understand it, to gain *insight* into it.
- Whenever possible, try to turn ideas and facts into mental pictures and/or rough cartoons.
- Mnemonic devices, self-constructed, are an effective way to remember general facts—list, names, and dates.

15

UNDERSTANDING YOUR INSTRUCTORS

Professors Are Human Beings Too

Where does an instructor go late at night, when the sun goes down and the day's work is done, when even evening classes have all been taught, when it's near midnight, when the world is asleep and the moon is full? The answer seems obvious, doesn't it?

Like the characters in a Stephen King novel, or an episode of the "Twilight Zone," it turns out that instructors aren't quite real. Instead of going to ordinary houses and apartments like yours, they secretly file, unobserved, to filing cabinets in a large subterranean room below the administration building. Each instructor occupies a single cabinet and is stored away something like a dormant vampire. In the morning, with refreshed rechargeable batteries, the reawakened instructors ascend in elevators to deliver predictable lectures from little tape recorders stored in their heads.

The above fantasy is, of course, ridiculous. We all know that instructors are *alive*, that they have thoughts and feelings like all human beings.

But this is merely an abstract knowledge. At a gut, or emotional, level there is often such a wide gap between a college instructor and a student that the student does in fact find it difficult to perceive the instructor as a three-dimensional person.

The mirror image of the error identified above can also be made by instructors when they forget that students are persons with individual differences. It is unfortunately true that there is a tendency for people, instructors or students, to see others as "objects" or "things" in the perceiving individual's psychological world. The theologian Martin Buber called relationships based on this unfortunate tendency, *I–it relationships*. When the humanity of another person is fully recognized, the relationship becomes *I–thou*. And this, of course, is desirable.

Both instructors and students need to recognize each other's humanity. On the practical side, it will definitely help you succeed in college and become a more effective student if you understand something about the human side of academic life. It will also be of value for you to recognize different kinds of patterns in teaching styles. And more, you need to know how to cope with them. As is often said, "It helps to be able to 'psych out' your instructor."

NOT ROBOTS, BUT HUMAN BEINGS

As the introduction to this chapter suggests, instructors are not robots but human beings. They have thoughts and feelings just as you do. To be more specific, they often worry about love relationships, marriages, children, money, health, and so forth. Just because they have a teaching position doesn't mean that they're "home free." Life is life. And it goes on no matter what your status, income, or age.

I am going to allow you to jump the fence between instructor and student and get a glimpse of the other side, a side you seldom see if you are not yourself an academician. A few examples will make clear the general point that instructors are human beings.

I have known instructors who . . .

. . . have had two or more marriages and several love affairs.

. . . can't pay their bills because they don't know how to manage money.

. . . bicker constantly with their spouses.

. . . are alienated from their children.

. . . think of their students as dull clods lacking in intelligence and imagination.

. . . are compulsive gamblers.

. . . teach English literature and seldom read novels.

. . . are burned out and now wish they had never gone into the teaching profession.

. . . feel sorry for themselves because "teachers are so poorly paid."

. . . think of themselves as losers because everyone "knows" that "Those who can *do*, and those who can't *teach*."

These examples are cited not to show that "the gods have clay feet" but to show that instructors are subject to all of the woes and worries of humankind.

One of the best stories written by the Russian author Anton Chekhov is called *A Dreary Story*. (It is also sometimes published under the title *A Boring Story*.) Written almost one hundred years ago, it tells the tale of an aging professor in a medical school. He is disenchanted with his wife of many years, disappointed in his children, unfulfilled in his profession, and unable to save a self-destructive young woman from herself. It provides a powerful glimpse into the negative aspects of a "successful" outer career. And the insights it provides are as applicable to the teaching profession today as they were in Chekhov's day. If you want to get a sober glimpse into the human side of a professor's life, read Chekhov's story.

THE ACADEMIC LIFE

The academic life, like any other calling, has its rewards, challenges, and disappointments. This section describes what it is like to instruct at the college level. Consequently, it will help you attain a better understanding of the human side of teaching. And if you are considering going into teaching yourself, it will give you a glimpse into a world usually unseen by students.

First, let's make a distinction among four words that overlap and have similar meanings. Their usage is subject to confusion and requires clarification. These words are *teacher, instructor, teaching assistant*, and *professor*. Obviously, the words teacher and instructor can be used more or less interchangeably. Nonetheless, it is important to consider the connotations, associations, and emotional links that go with a word. The word *teacher* usually suggests an individual who works with children from kindergarten all the way up to the twelvth grade. It also, of course, includes individuals who work with preschoolers. The word *instructor* implies an individual who teaches at the college level but who does not have academic rank. An instructor often teaches on a full-time contract but may have probationary status. The word *teaching assistant* implies a graduate student who is working toward a master's degree or a doctorate.

Part-time teaching at an hourly rate helps the student defray the costs of higher education. Working as a teaching assistant is seen as a kind of subsidy of the student's education.

The word *professor* implies an individual who has academic rank. The term *academic rank* itself suggests that the individual has a secure position and a certain degree of status among faculty peers. Academic rank in most colleges is formal, and the individual in question has a rank of assistant professor, associate professor, or full professor. Academic rank is not granted on the basis of time served in the profession alone, but rather it is based on merit. In a two-year community college, academic rank is earned by committee work, community work, and excellence as a teacher. In a four-year college, academic rank is earned not only by the activities already cited, but also by publications. These must be scholarly in nature, be published in recognized journals or by an academic press, and make a genuine contribution to the advancement of academic knowledge in a well-defined field of study.

In order to earn a permanent position, or *tenure*, at a four-year college it is essential to publish. This is where the famous phrase "publish or perish" comes from. If the would-be professor doesn't have the creativity and the ability to do scholarly research, he or she will be dismissed after a few years. Excellence in teaching, at a four-year college, is not enough to earn tenure for the individual.

The typical teaching load at a community college is 15 units (on the semester system). This means that the instructor is in class, actually lecturing or supervising a lab, 15 hours a week. A typical contract calls for an additional five posted office hours. During these times the instructor is expected to be available to students for questions, brief discussions, make-up examinations, and other special needs. More hours are required in order to prepare and grade examinations, serve on committees, and so forth. All in all, the average community college instructor puts in a solid 40-hour week.

The typical teaching load at a four-year college or a graduate school is six to nine units on the semester system. This sounds like a very light workload, but it is not. Remember that the instructor at this level is expected to be a genuine scholar, to do research, and to publish. This can be very stressful and demanding. So instructors at the higher academic levels, again, put in a solid forty-hour week or more.

How much do instructors earn on an annual basis? This varies greatly. With many colleges currently feeling a budget crunch, a number of instructors are hired on a part-time basis. These individuals do not have tenure, do not receive health benefits, and are not part of a college retirement plan. They are a financial bargain to the college because they are paid sometimes as little as one-third or one-half the pay that full-time instructors earn. Working sometimes at two or three colleges in an area in order to collect a full-time teaching load, the part-time instructor can expect to earn about $15,000 to $20,000 per year.

A beginning instructor with a contract and a master's degree can expect to earn between $25,000 and $30,000 per year. If the beginning instructor has a doctorate, starting pay will be about $30,000 to $35,000 per year. With academic rank and publications, pay can rise to $45,000 to $50,000 per year. A full professor, with publications and a number of years of experience, can expect to earn as much as $60,000 to $80,000 per year. This is a professor who is at the top of the academic ladder.

It is important to realize that some instructors have excellent opportunities to supplement their salaries. Working as a consultant on a part-time basis for corporations is one way to do this. Expert advice given on accounting practices, real estate, mathematics, engineering, architecture, and so forth is worth money. Another way in which salaries are supplemented is by the writing of textbooks, something that is not considered scholarly. It is not original or novel in nature because the information in a textbook represents a consensus of current knowledge. Textbook writing is an extension of teaching. It can be quite lucrative, and it is not at all unusual for a professor to earn royalties of $10,000 to $20,000 per year from a textbook. There are a few, perhaps only 5 percent of all textbook authors, who make as much as $50,000 to $100,000 in royalties in a single year from an outstanding textbook.

Much more could be said about the academic life. However, what has been said gives you some facts about the vocation of teaching at a college level. And it permits you to catch a glimpse of life on the other side of the college fence. College teaching is not a bed of roses. On the other hand, it is a rewarding vocation for those who are suited for it.

THE FIVE BASIC TEACHING STYLES

There are five basic teaching styles that are used, consciously or unconsciously, by all instructors. The styles arise from individual differences in traits of personality. They are caused more by an instructor's temperament than by his or her academic training or teacher education. Usually, a given instructor will manifest one basic style as a dominant tendency. Although instructors may briefly display any style, there is one that is, so to speak, home base.

It will help you greatly to be able to recognize and identify the styles. In the next section I'll suggest ways in which you can cope with the negative aspects of the styles. These will become personal survival strategies of the utmost importance in your student survival kit.

As a overview, it is worth noting that the five styles arise from two basic dimensions. These dimensions are said to be *bipolar* because opposite ends of the dimensions represent extreme flip-flops in style. The first dimension is called *authoritarian-permissive*. The second dimension is called *rejecting-accepting*. Imagine the two dimensions set like crosshairs in a telescopic sight. Let the East-West hair, or dimension, be the authoritarian-permissive one. Let the North-South hair, or dimension, be the rejecting-accepting one.

The above scheme automatically generates four extreme styles: (1) authoritarian-rejecting, (2) authoritarian-accepting, (3) permissive-rejecting, and (4) permissive-accepting. Where the dimensions intersect there is a fifth and last style: democratic-accepting.

The Authoritarian-Rejecting Style

The *authoritarian-rejecting* style is the most austere one. In terms of its authoritarian aspect, the instructor is overcontrolling and bossy and seems to have all of the answers. In terms of its rejecting aspect, the instructor is cold and remote. The instructor doesn't like the students much and makes this known in various indirect ways such as a haughty tone of voice, an arrogant facial expression, and a stiff body posture; he or she generally talks over the heads of most students. There is little respect for the students' views, and they are aware of it. The authoritarian rejecting style is the traditional one of the *pedagogue*, the "high-and-mighty" professor, the full-time know-it-all.

The authoritarian-rejecting style does not bring out the best in students because they often feel inferior and in academic water that is much too deep. Also, they feel alienated—disconnected—from the instructor. There is very little recognition given by the instructor for student effort. Consequently, student motivation often sinks to a generally low level.

The Authoritarian-Accepting Style

The *authoritarian-accepting* style is an improvement over the first style, but not much. In terms of its authoritarian aspect, the instructor is still overcontrolling and may make many arbitrary, nit-picking demands on students, but the students tend to feel liked. They will sometimes willingly jump through silly academic hoops for instructors who manifest the authoritarian-accepting style.

An important drawback of this second style is that the student is required to do very little critical thinking. A kind of blind, puppy-dog devotion to the all-knowing, all-wise, all-kind instructor may develop. This style fosters a dependent attitude that is at odds with the highest ideals of college teaching. The authoritarian-accepting style tends to foster a passive "feed-me-the-information" attitude.

The Permissive-Rejecting Style

The *permissive-rejecting* style is probably the most contradictory of the five styles. In terms of its permissive aspect, the message is, "I'm not at all certain of my ideas. I, the instructor, and you, the student, are all seekers of truth and knowledge together. We all share in the learning experience. I can learn from you as you learn from me." The instructor will ask vague, unanswerable essay questions that send out messages such as "be creative" or "anything goes." Chaos seems to reign supreme. The student at first feels that he or she has entered a magical kingdom of fascinating ideas and self-discovery.

Contradiction arises in terms of the style's rejecting aspect. Students find that their questions are ridiculed and their best ideas are met with scorn. The message conveyed, usually implicitly by facial expression or tone of voice, is, "You're an inferior intellect." The beleaguered student is in a double bind, a lose-lose situation. All attempts to please the instructor, who seems superficially to be flexible and open, are met with defeat and poor grades. The student is left shadow boxing and fanning academic air.

The Permissive-Accepting Style

The *permissive-accepting* style is, superficially, the "nicest" of the five styles. At the permissive level, the instructor allows great latitude for individual differences. There are very few rules and regulations. Perhaps attendance is not required. The instructor is an easy grader, hating to give any student, even incompetent ones, a D or an F for the semester. At the accepting level, the instructor has what the psychologist Carl Rogers called *unconditional positive regard* for the students. They are liked, almost loved, just because they exist. It *is* very pleasant to be a student in the presence of an instructor who exudes the permissive-accepting style.

Drawbacks of the style are several. First, the student is not challenged. The teaching tends to be sloppy. Concepts, terms, and facts are slighted in favor of vague abstractions. Second, the student leaves the class with the false impression that he or she has learned something, when in fact the class has been basically a pastime, a kind of entertainment. If the class is a prerequisite, then a second class in the same subject may be excessively difficult because the student is underprepared. Third, this style encourages a kind of mental laziness—a sort of "any idea I have is okay" attitude. The capacity for critical thinking is done a disservice. An instructor who favors the permissive-accepting style is like the Pied Piper of Hamelin, leading students down pathways that go nowhere in particular.

The Democratic-Accepting Style

The *democratic-accepting* style is the optimal one. The democratic aspect of the style suggests a region on the permissive-authoritarian dimension that is midway between the two extreme poles. The democratic instructor presents information with clarity and confidence, but not dogmatically. Discussion is encouraged. The general impression conveyed is sometimes said to be *authoritative*, not authoritarian. There is a relaxed attitude toward information and an openness to ideas offered by students. Moreover, the openness is sincere, not a pose adopted to patronize students.

At the accepting level, the instructor gives the impression to students that they are liked and respected. This status must to some degree be earned, however. If a student talks during a lecture, comes in late on a regular basis, or is otherwise irresponsible, the instructor is quick to inform the student that his or her behavior is unacceptable. This is done in a courteous manner, and there's no attack on the student's personality. Instead of moralizing, the instructor simply lets the student know what must be done.

There is no drawback to the democratic-accepting style. It is the one that fosters the greatest amount of learning. And it helps members of the class develop self-esteem as students. It is the style that should be encouraged in teacher training courses. A substantial body of research in educational psychology supports these statements.

The well-known novel *Goodbye, Mr. Chips* by James Hilton presents a portrait of an instructor who starts his career with an authoritarian-rejecting approach to students. This arises from his inexperience, and also from a somewhat rigid, introverted personality. Through a marriage to a loving, big-hearted woman he is transformed. Toward the end of the novel we see Mr. Chips as a democratic-accepting teacher, beloved by both his peers and his students. As a novice teacher he is portrayed as inconsequential and ineffective, but as an older teacher he is competent and effective. The contrast between the aging, demoralized professor in Chekhov's *Dreary Story* and the elderly, inspiring Mr. Chips is striking indeed.

COPING WITH THE FIVE STYLES

You will take about 40 courses (on the semester system) in order to graduate from college with a four-year degree. Allowing for the fact that you may sometimes have the same instructor twice and, infrequently, three times, you will probably be exposed to a total of about thirty different instructors. Be prepared to encounter all five of the basic styles more than once. And be prepared to cope with them. Forewarned is forearmed. Below are presented specific coping strategies that will help you deal competently with various kinds of instructors.

Coping with the Authoritarian-Rejecting Style

If an instructor manifests an authoritarian-rejecting style, you must become as flexible and adaptable as possible. You have to bend to the style in somewhat the same way that a new recruit needs to to bend—or break—in the presence of a drill instructor. There is no sense in raging and expecting the instructor magically to change to meet your needs. He or she has the power, whether you like it or not. And a distasteful teaching style is not a basis for a student grievance or a complaint to the instructor's department head. The name of the game is *survival*, your survival.

The key to survival with an authoritarian-rejecting instructor is to give the instructor *what he or she wants*. Usually this will be obvious and specific. This type of instructor is organized and legalistic. You *do* have to obey all of the little rules set down, but if you do, you *will* learn something and you will pass the course.

Let the instructor be the boss. Adapt. Comply. And resist the temptation to drop the course. Dropping courses is time consuming and expensive. Often the authoritarian-rejecting instructor lets up a bit as the course winds toward its end. And you will find out that by studying hard and playing by his or her rules you'll probably come out all right in the long run.

Coping with the Authoritarian-Accepting Style

If an instructor manifests an authoritarian-accepting style, you may very well find yourself greatly admiring him or her. Survival in the course is relatively easy. All you have to do is to meet the course requirements, and there is unlikely to arise within you a state of distress and mental conflict. The primary risk is subtle. It will seem that the instructor is absolutely right about almost everything. Resist the temptation to be overly influenced. Keep your own counsel and privately, at a mental level, challenge the instructor's ideas. Try to preserve your autonomy. At a practical, behavioral level, however, coping with the authoritarian-accepting style presents no great problem. You can pass the course readily by following the instructor's guidelines, which are usually quite explicit.

Coping with the Permissive-Rejecting Style

If the instructor manifests a permissive-rejecting style, you have your hands full. The permissive aspect of the style is likely to make you baffled and confused. Instruction is indefinite and ambiguous. You try to "read" the instructor and fail. *It's not your fault.* Because the instructor is rejecting, *nothing* you do will really please him or her. I don't blame you if you drop the class, because sometimes this is your only way out. Take the same subject from another instructor. I don't like to give this advice, because, as I said earlier, dropping classes is time consuming and expensive. An alternative is to "tough it out," which many students do. However, if on the basis of two or three examinations or assignments, you project a poor semester grade, then dropping the class is a good final option.

You can't really win with instructors who employ a permissive-rejecting style. They are the most frustrating and difficult kind of instructor to deal with in the entire array I have been describing.

Coping with the Permissive-Accepting Style

The instructor who manifests a permissive-accepting style is relatively easy to deal with. You won't know for sure what you are supposed to do or what the instructor wants, but, in a sense, so what? Almost any effort you make will be rewarded and recognized. You can't lose. This kind of instructor tends to be an easy grader. On the negative side you may not learn much, but you will not find it difficult to earn a fairly high grade, and credits toward graduation, without too much effort. Of all of the styles discussed, including the democratic-accepting one, the permissive-accepting one makes the fewest demands on you.

Coping with the Democratic-Accepting Style

If the instructor manifests a democratic-accepting style, thank your lucky stars. You will learn something because the course will have structure and well-defined objectives within a flexible framework. Your work and assignments will be fairly graded. What you need to do as a student is to follow the guidelines and strategies already outlined in this book. Do your part and meet the instructor halfway, and you can expect to succeed in the course.

As I hope is clear from the above discussion, it is important to "read" your instructor and identify his or her dominant teaching style. Then you can adopt the appropriate coping strategy, the one that will maximize your likelihood of success as a student.

CONCLUDING REMARKS

It is quite within the realm of possibility that you may find yourself in a class offered by an instructor who is younger than you are. It is not at all unusual for someone to have earned a master's degree by the age of twenty-two or twenty-three. Graduate students working as teaching assistants, or TAs, may be younger. You will be tempted to think such thoughts, depending on your own age, as, "She's just a child!," "I have a son his age," "What can she possibly know about life?" or "I wonder if he shaves yet?" Well, go ahead and think your thoughts. Indulge yourself. But don't let prejudicial propositions cloud your judgment.

If the instructor is standing before you, then he or she is *academically qualified.* No matter how youthful that person appears to be, this is an individual with a degree who has passed not one but *several* courses in the subject matter that is being taught. Adopt an interested attitude and realize that, although the instructor may have much to learn about life in general, he or she probably has a lot to teach about a specific subject such as physics, algebra, or sociology.

KEY POINTS TO REMEMBER

- It will help you succeed in college and become a more effective student if you understand something about the human side of academic life.
- Instructors are not robots but human beings. They have thoughts, worries, and feelings just like you do.
- The words *teacher, instructor, teaching assistant,* and *professor* have different connotations, associations, and emotional links.

- The term *academic rank* suggests that the individual has a secure position and a certain degree of status among faculty peers.
- An instructor or professor with *tenure* has a permanent position.
- The typical teaching load at a community college is 15 units (on the semester system). The typical teaching load at a four-year college or a graduate school is 6 to 9 units.
- A beginning contract instructor can expect to earn between $25,000 and $30,000 per year. A full professor may earn as much as $60,000 to $80,000 per year.
- The *authoritarian-rejecting* style is characterized by these traits: controlling, bossy, cold, and remote. The key to coping with this style is to bend to it, becoming as flexible and adaptable as possible.
- The *authoritarian-accepting* style is characterized by these traits: controlling, bossy, warm, and kind. Coping with this style presents no great problem. You can pass the course easily by following the instructors's guidelines, which are usually quite explicit.
- The *permissive-rejecting* style is characterized by these traits: lack of structure, absence of well-defined learning goals, cold, and remote. This is the most difficult style to cope with. Your alternatives are to "tough it out" or to drop out. You can't really win with instructors who employ this style.
- The *permissive-accepting* style is characterized by these traits: lack of structure, absence of well-defined learning goals, warm, and kind. It is relatively easy to cope with this style. Even if you are confused and unsure of what to do, you will not find it difficult to earn a fairly high grade without too much effort.
- The *democratic-accepting* style is the optimal one. It is characterized by these traits: clarity of presentations, lack of a dogmatic attitude, openness to ideas, and respect for students. This style presents no need for a specific coping strategy. You should simply try to be an effective student, following the guidelines and strategies already outlined in this book.
- If your instructor is younger than you are, keep in mind that he or she is *academically qualified.* Consequently, adopt an open, interested attitude toward instruction.

16

COPING WITH YOUR FAMILY

You Can't Please Them All

You want the members of your family to support you in your college career. Unfortunately, this is frequently not the case. Simple unconditional acceptance of your academic goals may not be forthcoming.

Probably others will not be dead set against what you want to do, but they will be *ambivalent*, feeling both positive and negative attitudes toward your student role. You will have to sell the role. Don't be defensive about this. Why should anybody buy anything, including your dreams and ambitions, without knowing the contents within the package being presented?

Let's explore ways in which your family can hinder—or help—your desire to be a college student.

INTIMATE ANTAGONISTS

I am going to assume in this section that you are married or in a committed relationship. Instead of the term *spouse*, I will employ the more general word *partner* to indicate what is known as your "significant other."

You have finally decided to go back to school! Isn't that wonderful? I think so, or I wouldn't have written this book. I'm delighted that although you are over 25 and an adult with responsibilities you want to meet new challenges and make the most of your life.

But I am not your partner.

Maybe your partner has some doubts. Why can't he or she be "understanding" and "loving" and "supportive" and all of those other wonderful things you read about in magazines? Well, let's examine it from your partner's point of view.

Let's say you are female and your partner is male. How do things look from his point of view? There are a set of potential negatives associated with your going to school. These include loss of income, extra expenses, the feeling of being neglected, less energy and interest on your part in sexual relations, more child-rearing responsibilities, inferior meals, clothes that aren't washed and ironed, and so forth. He perceives your return to school not as a pleasant dream but as a kind of nightmare in which he is the loser.

You, of course, must provide him with reassurance that his worst fears won't come true. And you had better make good on your promises. Let's face it—his fears are not completely unfounded.

Males in particular are unusually threatened when their partners go back to school. If they are members of the "working class," they are often afraid that their partners will "rise above them." If a man is a truck driver, a plumber, or a short-order cook, he may not be particularly delighted to be married to a woman who has become a nurse, teacher, certified public accountant, or who has otherwise acquired a profession. If he is a traditional male, his ego may be greatly threatened. His usually dominant role as the more knowing, the more powerful member of a partnership has been knocked over. And he feels knocked over too. It takes a male with a strong ego to cope with this kind of a situation.

An additional problem is that he may fear that while you are in college you may be attracted to other men you meet. And jealousy rears its ugly head.

Now let's turn things around and say that your partner is female. You, the male, are the college student. How do things look from her point of view? Generally, women's egos do not feel threatened if their men acquire more formal education than they have. But there are other risks. A woman may work full time, take care of the house or apartment, wash laundry and do most of the cooking and child rearing while her partner takes classes and studies. This has been called, among other things, "putting hubby through" or "putting my man through."

After all the work and sacrifice, the female may "get dumped" for another woman. If this happens, the first partner is not only emotionally bereft, she has been financially hit as well. The male goes on to a new relationship and a high-paying vocation or profession. She is stuck and has thrown away precious years in a bad investment. The fear that this worst-case scenario may actually come true often dampens a female partner's commitment to her male partner's higher education.

It is, consequently, for good reason that some marriage counselors have called husbands and wives, or committed partners, *intimate antagonists*. They are emotionally close, but they also oppose each other in important ways.

Going to college may aggravate bickering and fighting, driving couples apart. It is important to seek effective ways to diminish the impact of the kinds of negative factors that will both undermine a relationship and have an adverse effect on academic performance.

Let's pursue a deeper understanding of the kinds of patterns that develop when people are intimate antagonists. This can include not only partners but also children and parents.

GAMES FAMILIES PLAY

Eric Berne, father of a kind of psychotherapy known as Transactional Analysis (TA) and author of the book *Games People Play*, realized that people in families often engage in self-defeating and self-destructive patterns of social interaction. Because interpersonal relationships are often competitive and predictable, Berne called them *games*. A closer look at some specific games will help you avoid being spun about by them.

You Always Hold Me Back

A game that you are likely to play as a student is called *You Always Hold Me Back*. You initiate the game by accusing your partner of standing in your way, not caring about the importance of actualizing your potential, and placing blocks in the road leading to an academic career. Your partner insists that all of your claims are false. Nonetheless, your partner recognizes at an intuitive level, because of your nonverbal, psychological messages, that you *want* to be held back. You use the game to provide a rationalization for failure. It helps you avoid the challenges and psychological risk associated with being a student.

If your partner has an authoritarian personality, he or she will foolishly take the bait. This means that he or she *will* insist that you devote more time to the demands of the marriage and otherwise place roadblocks in your path. In effect, your partner has become your patsy. But you will decide that he or she is the villain of the piece, denying to yourself that you have created the situation.

It is necessary to take a big psychological step back and look at the game in objective terms. You can break out of the game by deciding that you *are not* going to set up a rationalization for failure by self-indulgently initiating a game of You Always Hold Me Back. Instead, calmly let your partner know what you want to do in terms of a college education. Know your own mind; be definite, realistic, and rational; adopt the student role on a gradual basis; take only one or two classes your first semester in college; and prove to yourself and your partner that going to school *can* work, and that it doesn't have to upset the apple cart of your relationship. In this way you won't trigger an authoritarian, overcontrolling response— a response that will greatly interfere with your academic aspirations.

Mommy Doesn't Love Us Anymore

Let's say that you are a mother. Your child or children may resent the fact that you are going to school. Frequently children are jealous of the time that you give to classes and to studying, time that you could very well be giving to them. They may feel that your emotional investment in your college career is greater than your emotional investment in them. These feelings on the part of children may induce them to play a game with you that can be called *Mommy Doesn't Love Us Anymore*.

At this point, you may be wondering why there isn't a parallel game called *Daddy Doesn't Love Us Anymore*. The reason is that, as unfair as it is, children feel no sense of abandonment when a father goes to college. It is the expected, traditional role of men to spend a lot of time out of the house. And if a mother is employed and earning money, being out of the house is seen as necessary, as a requirement associated with her job. But going to college? This is a *choice*, or at least it is perceived as one by children. And they can easily conclude that you are choosing college over them.

The way in which children play *Mommy Doesn't Love Us Anymore* is by finding various ways to sabotage your educational goals. They may "get sick" so that *you* have to stay away from school in order to care for them. Or they may whine, complain, become uncooperative, get bad grades, and so forth. These are a set of *passive-aggressive* behaviors designed to get at you without making a frontal attack. Children don't usually have the self-confidence or the clarity of perception of the situation to confront you directly, negotiate, and reason logically. Instead, probably unconsciously, they seek to make you *feel guilty*. And the tactic may very well work. More than one mother has abandoned college work because she "can't go to school and be a good mother."

The first thing you have to do in coping with *Mommy Doesn't Love Us Anymore* is to realize that the game exists and that it *is* a game. You must say to yourself, and it is no rationalization, that in the long run acquiring more education can easily make you a better mother. You will be a self-actualizing person, not a bored, frustrated one, and you will *add* to the enrichment of your children's lives. Having decided this, you must make it a point to set aside time for your children. Take one course less this semester if you have to. Make plans and follow through on your promises. Give the children something to look forward to—little things like eating out at a family restaurant, going to a movie, or taking a walk together. Reassurance with words is not enough. You must *show* by your deeds that you have not abandoned them emotionally.

This can be done in interactions that take only a few minutes. For example, let's say that five-year-old Gina interrupts you while you're studying and says, "Mommy, I can't find my toothbrush." If you say in a harsh tone of voice, "Don't bother me now, I'm studying," the child will get the message that the books are more important than she is, and she'll feel discounted. On the other hand, if you take a few minutes out to search for the toothbrush, the child will feel reassured, and maybe a need for such reassurance was the real motive behind the request.

Responding in the way described above requires not so much time as it does flexibility. You must be able to break off and pick up your college work without too much aggravation or frustration. I know this can be hard, but you are trying to wear two caps: mother and college student. And it was your choice to take on the dual role. So work on being flexible. It will pay off; you will feel that you are a responsible mother, and your children will not need to play *Mommy Doesn't Love Us Anymore* with you.

You're Never Going to Amount to Anything

You're Never Going to Amount to Anything is a game played by parents who have grown to be disappointed in their children. The parents' own dreams and plans for their children have failed to materialize. Perhaps they are bitterly disappointed. When you, now an adult, approach them and announce that you are going back to school, that you are enrolling in college, they may give a mental groan and think, "Another wild goose chase. Another dead end."

If you ask them for financial assistance or help with child care, the help may be given, but in a grudging resentful way. And you will be resentful in turn, thinking, "Why can't they believe in me? Why can't they have a little faith?"

You must realize that they feel very much like the people who heard the boy who cried "wolf." They have lost faith because there have been too many false alarms. If your parents' response to your educational aspirations is less than enthusiastic, you can understand why. They don't perceive a history of success, and, consequently, don't project success in the future.

Try to understand them. They hesitate to make an emotional investment in your educational dreams because they don't want to get hurt. In a sense, they don't *dare* to dream. They are protecting themselves from disappointment.

You can cope with the game by deciding *not* to argue with them, *not* to try to convince them in words that you merit their emotional support. Instead, calmly proceed toward your educational goals. Move in a positive direction on your own. You don't *need* their approval. If you think you do, you are unnecessarily casting yourself in the child's role. You *are* an adult, at least at a biological level, although it is of course easy to "become" a child again when you are in the presence of your parents.

In a nutshell, *earn* your parents' respect by your actual accomplishments. If you go to college and make a success of it, they'll stop playing *You're Never Going to Amount to Anything.*

USING ASSERTIVENESS SKILLS

You can more readily enlist the cooperation of your family, and get them to stop playing games, if you use *assertiveness skills.* These are a set of specific communication strategies arising from research on behavior therapy. The assertive response to another person is the "ideal" response between a passive one and an aggressive one. A *passive* response is a wishy-washy one in which you end up feeling used and abused. An *aggressive* response is a hostile one in which you end up alienating others and pushing them away from you. The assertive response lets you stand up for your rights in a rational, firm manner. Its effect, if done properly, should not be offensive to another person.

Listed below are five well-defined assertiveness skills that will help you cope effectively with your family.

1. *Feeling talk.* Feeling talk is a skill in which you state your position or desires with an appropriate degree of emotion. You can say to your partner "I want to become a nurse" in a flat, thin, unconvincing, almost inaudible voice. Or you can make the same statement in a fully audible, convincing voice. You can emphasize the word *want* in the sentence, conveying a degree of passion. Your partner is more likely to take your statement seriously if the feeling tone associated with it is appropriate.

2. *Don't discount your partner's objections.* Assume your partner says, "I don't see how we can make it financially if you go to college." Don't respond with, "Oh, that's just like you. Always looking at the negative side of things." Instead, take the objection seriously. Say, "I know what you're getting at, but I've thought it through. And here's how I think we can work it out." And proceed to offer some ideas that will lead to a constructive discussion.

3. *Be concrete.* Don't talk about your academic goals in vague abstractions. Your partner will feel you are just wandering around, groping in the dark. Avoid saying, "I'm thinking of taking some classes and maybe I'll get a profession or something." Instead say, "I'm going to sign up for an accounting class. I'm interested in looking into accounting as a possible vocation. You know I've always enjoyed working with numbers."

4. *Broken record.* You may have to state a desire more than once before a member of your family takes you seriously. Repetition is a basic way that messages get through. Using the skill called *broken record*, you state your position calmly, but with *conviction*, a number of times until the other person is reached. For example, the first time you say you are going to become a college student your partner may laugh and say that's silly. The tenth time you say it, he or she won't think it's so silly and will know that you mean it.

5. *Speak from your adult self.* Your adult self is the rational side of your personality. If a member of your family frustrates you, it is tempting to act and speak from the child self, the emotional side of your personality. When this happens, you may allow yourself to be browbeaten and say in a defeated, weak voice, "Well, maybe you're right." Or you may get your dander up and say in an angry voice, "You don't care about me! You want to hold me back! I would think that you would want me to get more education. Well, you've just

shown me your true colors." Instead, stay focused. Ask yourself, "How would my adult-self act and speak in this situation?" Reflect and delay your response. And then speak in the way that you associate with your adult-self.

Employing the five assertiveness skills listed will go a long way toward helping you cope with your family. As the subtitle of the chapter says, "You can't please them all." But you can make a realistic effort to elicit a maximum amount of understanding and cooperation.

CONCLUDING REMARKS

Yes, your family can interfere with the pursuit of your academic goals, but your family can also be your greatest source of emotional support. When there is a graduation ceremony, who is there in the audience clapping and wearing big happy smiles? And who is taking pictures during and following the ceremony? Why, it's the members of your family, of course. More often than not you will see the proud graduate surrounded by equally proud partners, children, and parents.

Apply the suggestions offered in this chapter, and do your best to make your family an ally in your efforts to reach your educational goals.

KEY POINTS TO REMEMBER

- Members of your family are likely to be *ambivalent* concerning your student role, having both positive and negative attitudes toward it.
- Potential negatives experienced by a male when a female partner goes back to school include a threatened ego, loss of income, the feeling of being neglected, less energy and interest on her part in sexual relations, and more child-rearing responsibilities for him.
- Potential losses experienced by a female when a male partner goes back to school include being overburdened with a job, child care, and housework. In addition, there is the threat that the female may eventually "get dumped" for another woman.
- Husbands and wives, or committed partners, have been called *intimate antagonists* by some marriage counselors. They are emotionally close, but they also oppose each other in important ways.
- People in families often engage in *games*, predictable self-defeating and self-destructive patterns of social interaction.

- *You Always Hold Me Back* is a game in which you, the student, accuse a partner of standing in your way, of not caring about the importance of actualizing your potential.
- *Mommy Doesn't Love Us Anymore* is a game in which children oppose your student role, often in passive-aggressive ways, in order to elicit demonstrations of love from you.
- *You're Never Going to Amount to Anything* is a game played by parents who have grown disappointed in their children. The aim of the game is to protect the parents from more disappointments.
- *Assertiveness skills* are communication skills that help you stand up for your rights and gain the long-term cooperation of your family.
- *Feeling talk* requires that you state your position or desires concerning higher education with an appropriate degree of emotion.
- *Not discounting* requires that you take your partner's statements and objections to a college career seriously.
- *Being concrete* requires that you avoid using vague abstractions when talking about your academic goals and plans.
- *Broken record* requires that you calmly repeat a message until it gets through to your partner and he or she realizes that you mean what you say about your education.
- *Speaking from your adult self* requires that you state your point of view concerning your academic plans in logical, rational terms.

17

GETTING AHEAD

The Art of Self Realization

Examine the two words in the main title of this chapter—*getting ahead*. What do they mean to you? Does getting ahead refer to financial gain, making more money than you are making now? Or does getting ahead refer to making the most of your talents and potentialities, becoming the person you were meant to be?

In order to get ahead do you have to "sell your soul for pottage," give up your fondest personal dreams for the almighty dollar? Some writers who have thought about the matter seem to suggest that this is so. George Orwell, eminent author of *1984*, wrote a lesser-known novel called *Keep the Aspidistra Flying*. In this book a young man with literary talent gives up his higher aspirations in order to compose advertising copy. In order to get married and have a middle-class standard of living he sells out to what he calls the "Money-God."

On the other hand, if getting ahead means to bring to fruition your talents, do you have to become something like a "starving artist"? Paul Gauguin, the French Impressionist painter who abandoned a wife and four children and went to Tahiti in order to follow his star, is often cited as an example of the person who refused to sell out to the Establishment. The novel *The Moon and Sixpence* by W. Somerset Maugham is based on Gauguin's life.

The kind of either-or thinking about life's pathways represented by these two novels is logically fallacious. It is *not necessary* to make a choice between earning money and the proper use of your intelligence and creativity. On the contrary, you will probably make more money doing something you are good at, that you like doing, than something you force yourself to do to make a living. Working solely for money means doing "just a job," and you are likely to burn out early in your career. On the contrary, working at something you enjoy is a vocation, and you will be able to continue with it for many years.

One of the main purposes of college should be to help you discover your true vocation in life. Moreover, college should help you develop the skills that will help you make a success of that vocation.

WHAT IS YOUR TRUE VOCATION IN LIFE?

The root word from which *vocation* is derived is *vocare*, a Latin root meaning "to call." The original meaning was that an individual was personally called, or destined, to a certain profession, often a religious life. Some of the original meaning has been retained in our contemporary usage. A vocation is often spoken of as "a calling." The implication, very generally, is that we have a place, a mission, or a task in some grand plan of God or pattern of Nature.

Your "true vocation" is, in brief, what you are "meant to do" with your life. How do you discover your true vocation? For some people it is very easy. The great physicist Enrico Fermi, the first scientist to build an atomic pile capable of a controlled nuclear reaction, knew from an early age that he was destined for a career in mathematics and physics. He showed incredible talent in these fields of study and did not struggle against himself.

In today's culture, however, many people face what the psychoanalyst Erik Erikson called an *identity crisis*, a period of youthful struggle, starting in adolescence, characterized by a lack of a robust sense of self and uncertainty about one's true vocation. This common condition is probably caused by many social factors, including a bewildering set of confusing possible vocations and the opportunity, as this book so definitely states, to go to college at any age.

If you are suffering to some degree from an identity crisis, don't be too hard on yourself. Avoid self-criticism. I have been in your shoes, for I was about 30 years old before I was able to commit to a career focusing on teaching, and writing about, psychology. The only question that should really concern you is *how* do you resolve an identity crisis and discover your true vocation?

As I indicated in chapters 2 and 3, discussions with an academic counselor and the taking of vocational and aptitude tests can be helpful. It may be useful to keep a journal of thoughts and reflections. Ask yourself *on paper* questions such as: (1) What do I really want to do with my life? (2) Where am I going? (3) What do I really enjoy doing? Then answer the questions, again on paper. You may be pleasantly surprised to find that a real process of self-discovery is taking place.

And, of course, simply taking a few classes on a part-time basis at a local community college may help you become more aware of possible career opportunities and neglected personal interests. If you are in an identity crisis now, it will tend to resolve itself with experience and effort. I am reminded of a slow-to-develop film. It is placed in the developing solution but there seems to be no picture. It's *blank*. Or is it? Now the picture begins to emerge. Little by little it becomes sharp and clear. The picture was there all the time—but it took a little while to bring it out. Be patient and you will discover within yourself the "picture" for your life—your true vocation.

THE SELF-ACTUALIZING PROCESS

Abraham Maslow, a principal founder of humanistic psychology, asserted that one of the highest human motives is *self-actualization,* an inborn need to make the most of our talents and potentialities. It is this need that provides you with the enduring desire to find your true vocation in life. You are, of course, encouraged to be self-actualizing. If you are not, in the long run you will be disappointed in yourself and in your life. This will make you prone to self-criticism and depression. Also, note that psychologists do not speak of *the* self-actualized person. Instead, they speak of the self-actualizing *process.* It is an ongoing series of events and is never complete. Applied to learning, one is never done. There are always new things to learn.

As noted above, you are encouraged to be self-actualizing. Note the emphasis on the word *self*. Self-actualization is, to some extent, egocentric. Let's assume that you are married and that you have children and responsibilities. You can't think only of self-actualization, which is essentially a process directed toward one person—you. You must also think in terms of the "We," of the family. This is the pathway of the traditional person. It is possible to conceptualize a *family-actualization* process, one in which the individual members pull for the success of the group, not themselves. A dramatic instance of this is provided by *The Grapes of Wrath* by John Steinbeck. In this novel, members of the Joad family place the welfare of the family above the welfare of its individual members. Each person struggles in his or her own way to help the family survive in its difficult move from Oklahoma to California during the Great Depression.

Fortunately, the process of self-actualization need not be at cross-purposes with the needs of your family. If an oppositional approach is taken, this can lead to distress, alienation, and divorce. It is far better to seek a compromise between egocentric needs and group needs, between *you* and your family. This way, the "middle way," is the win-win solution that serves each individual member in the family well.

OUR SEARCH FOR MEANING

As high as it is on the motivational ladder, self-actualization is not the highest human need. This is identified by existential philosophers and psychologists to be a *need for meaning* in life. The psychiatrist Viktor Frankl proposes that we have an inborn will to meaning. We want, we *need*, meaning in our lives in the same way that we want and need food. How do we satisfy the need for meaning?

The answer is by *discovering* positive values. For example, let's say you place great value on the happiness of your partner or on the welfare of your children. Whatever activities you engage in to promote their happiness or welfare will have value to you, and your life will have automatic meaning.

The same reasoning can be applied to your vocation. Let's say that in some way it promotes the happiness and welfare of other people. The vocation itself need not be esoteric. Almost every paying vocation—chef, nurse, physician, auto mechanic, and others—bestows benefits on others. If you enjoy your vocation, and work at it in a sincere, devoted way, then your vocation will have meaning to you.

It turns out that the end of our search for meaning resides not in the clouds but right here at the down-to-earth level.

DISCOVERING THE CREATIVE SELF

There is a tendency to look at our behavior as reactive—as the result of early experiences and life situations. If these are adverse, and they sometimes are, you can easily fall into the role of *victim*, the person who "can't win" because everyone and everything is against him or her.

I have tried to show in many ways in this book that you *have a choice*. You have more control and autonomy than you think you have. We all do. But you must grant to yourself a degree of personal power. Alfred Adler, a pioneer psychotherapist, spoke of the *Creative Self*, the self in all of us that can take charge of life, make positive decisions, and help us reach our goals.

Seek to discover your own Creative Self. Use it to escape from learned helplessness and other negative factors that may act as barriers to achievement. But more than that, use it to find the way to success as a responsible adult college student. At any age, this will be your pathway to getting ahead and to reaching your academic and vocational goals.

CONCLUDING REMARKS

Louisa May Alcott, author of *Little Women*, overcame many obstacles in order to make her mark as a writer. She wrote the following words of inspiration, which can be applied to almost any field of endeavor, including the challenges—and opportunities—of college: "Far away there in the sunshine are my highest aspirations. I may not reach them, but I can look up and see their beauty, believe in them, and try to follow where they lead."

KEY POINTS TO REMEMBER

- It is not necessary to make a choice between earning money and using your intelligence and creativity properly.
- The root word from which *vocation* is derived is *vocare*, a Latin root meaning "to call." Your "true vocation" is what you are "called to do" with your life.

- An *identity crisis* is a period of youthful struggle, starting in adolescence, characterized by lack of a robust sense of self and uncertainty about one's true vocation.
- Abraham Maslow asserted that one of the highest human motives is *self-actualization*, an inborn need to make the most of our talents and potentialities.
- It is possible to conceptualize a *family-actualization* process, one in which the individual members pull for the success of the group, not themselves.
- Viktor Frankl proposed that we have an inborn need to find meaning in life. This need can be satisfied by discovering positive values, tasks, and responsibilities worth doing.
- Alfred Adler spoke of the *Creative Self*, the self in all of us that can take charge of life, make positive decisions, and help us reach our goals.

18

QUIZ: ARE YOU READY TO GO BACK TO SCHOOL?

This chapter consists of a self-scoring examination that will help you evaluate (1) how much you have learned from this book and (2) your readiness to go back to school.

Part I is the test itself. It consists of true-false questions on every chapter. There is a total of one hundred questions. The test items deal with the basic terms and concepts presented in *Going Back to School*.

Part II is the answer key to the test. The answer key explains briefly why each answer is either true or false. The answers are keyed to pages in the book for easy reference.

Part III is a scoring guide.

PART I: EXAMINATION

Directions: Read each question and circle your answer, True or False.

Chapter 1: Going Back

1. College is only for unusually bright people.   T   F
2. It is possible to go to college even if you don't have a   T   F
   lot of free time.
3. You can go to college even if you don't have a lot of   T   F
   money.
4. You have to pass entrance examinations in order to go   T   F
   to college.

5. Although there are individual exceptions, college graduates tend to earn more money than non-college graduates.   T   F

Chapter 2: Before You Go Back

6. Community colleges are often referred to as *junior colleges* because they are seldom fully accredited institutions.   T   F

7. The typical college counselor is a member of the school's clerical staff who has been promoted to a higher position.   T   F

8. The college catalog is, in essence, the school's contract with you.   T   F

9. An alternative admissions program consists of a policy that allows applicants who do not come up to usual academic criteria to gain admission.   T   F

10. Tuition at a community college is, in most cases, free.   T   F

11. The vast majority of state-funded colleges and universities require full-time attendance.   T   F

Chapter 3: Getting In

12. General education courses count toward graduation. It is advisable to take ones that are somewhat related to your major.   T   F

13. If some of the classes in your proposed schedule are closed, it is probably best to not register right now but rather to wait and come back next semester.   T   F

14. The authority of the college catalog supersedes the authority of the counselor.   T   F

15. Placement tests are measurements of intelligence, creativity, and personality.   T   F

16. Let's say that you score in the 70th percentile on the Verbal Scale of the Scholastic Assessment Test (SAT). This means that, based on a standardized population of subjects who have already taken the test, you are above 70 percent of them. Or, put differently, you are in the top 30 percent.   T   F

17. The assumption that colleges make by requiring a wide range of general education courses is that you will not merely become a specialist but also an *educated person*.   T   F

Chapter 4: Staying In

18. The overall college success rate is encouraging.   T   F
    Probably somewhat more than 70% of people who attend
    college earn a four-year degree.

19. The high-risk student usually has a positive self-concept   T   F
    as a student.

20. If you lack academic direction, your counselor can   T   F
    arrange for you to take standardized tests that will help
    you decide on an academic major and eventual vocation.
    The two basic kinds of tests that are helpful are the
    Wechsler Adult Intelligence Scale (WAIS) and the
    Rorschach inkblot test.

21. An adult reentry center may offer short, optional classes   T   F
    in assertiveness training, stress reduction, behavior
    modification with children, and weight control.

22. Financial aid tends to fall into three broad categories: T   F
    scholarships, loans, and grants.

23. The academic adviser is somewhat different from the   T   F
    general counselor in the Counseling Office.

Chapter 5: How to Concentrate on a Textbook

24. There is no real distinction between reading a textbook   T   F
    and studying it.

25. Voluntary attention is the kind of attention in which you   T   F
    focus on information by an act of will.

26. Change of stimulation has no effect on attention.   T   F

27. SQ3R stands for study, question, recognize, reconstruct,   T   F
    and remember.

28. Fully 50 percent of your study time should be spent in   T   F
    recitation.

29. It is a bad idea to combine the SQ3R method with the   T   F
    use of flash cards.

Chapter 6: How People Learn

30. Learning is defined as a permanent change in thinking,   T   F
    perception, and memory as a result of cognitive reward.

31. The law of contiguity states that the basic process of   T   F
    learning involves connecting two or more stimuli.

32. You can use the classical conditioning process to your   T   F
    advantage by arranging that the cues, or conditioned
    stimuli, for your study behavior be unfamiliar, hard-to-
    obtain ones.

33. A specific application of operant conditioning to your   T   F
    study behavior calls for studying in small, well-defined
    units of behavior.

34. Insight exists when a mind can bring together formerly   T   F
    disconnected parts into an organized, meaningful whole.

35. Because of the learning-to-learn principle, your learning   T   F
    tasks become more difficult as you progress up the
    academic ladder.

36. There is research in learning theory suggesting that slow   T   F
    learning often results in better long-term retention of
    subject matter.

Chapter 7: Motivating Yourself

37. There is no distinction of importance to be made   T   F
    between the term *underachiever* and the term
    underachievement syndrome.

38. You may be blind to an underachievement syndrome in   T   F
    yourself because of an ego-defense mechanism known
    as *denial of reality*.

39. The lack of a well-defined identity can be a causal factor   T   F
    in underachievement.

40. It is rather far-fetched to suggest that poor nutrition can   T   F
    play a significant role in underachievement.

41. Unconscious motives in the form of "forbidden wishes"   T   F
    or desires that are prohibited by one's culture and family
    training can have an adverse impact on academic
    motivation.

42. Dreams and long-term goals are important incentives for   T   F
    behavior.

Chapter 8: Coping with Math Anxiety

43. Math anxiety can be defined as a tendency to feel fear   T   F
    and/or vague feelings of apprehension when one is trying
    to learn a mathematical concept, attempting to work a
    mathematical problem, or taking an examination.

44. A body of research evidence in educational psychology   T   F
    on how children learn mathematical concepts suggests
    that they need *concrete examples*, examples that include
    the actual handling of measuring instruments, the
    counting of markers on a rod, and the ordering of objects
    by size and shape.

45. Research suggests that the left hemisphere of the brain   T   F
    mediates such mental processes as verbal, logical, and
    mathematical thought.

46. The language of mathematics is nonredundant.   T   F

47. In coping with math anxiety, it is of little or no value to   T   F
    take advantage of the desensitization process.

48. If you have a mathematical inferiority complex that tells   T   F
    you that you are incompetent in mathematics, this means
    that you actually *are* incompetent.

Chapter 9: Organizing Your Time

49. The concept of time management is an illusion because   T   F
    it is impractical to think that one can learn to budget
    time in a rational manner.

50. The time-pressure syndrome consists of a set of positive   T   F
    and self-constructive attitudes and behaviors.

51. Perfectionism is the point of view that everything that   T   F
    one does must measure up to a nearly impossible
    standard of excellence.

52. An important skill associated with time management is   T   F
    assigning priorities to your tasks.

53. A schedule allows you to see a whole week from a   T   F
    bird's-eye view and makes it possible for you to find a
    Gestalt, a complete pattern or organized whole.

54. It is usually better to be time oriented than to be task   T   F
    oriented.

Chapter 10: Writing a Term Paper

55. In spite of academic rationalizations, a term paper is   T   F
    actually a kind of arbitrary harassment.

56. To say that your term paper must have a thesis is to say   T   F
    that it must make a point, it must have some central idea.

57. An example of a primary source of information would be   T   F
an encyclopedia article on the Old West.

58. The four basic stages in creative thinking are: T   F
(1) preparation, (2) incubation, (3) illumination, and
(4) verification.

59. The writing in a term paper should be a little ambiguous   T   F
and highly abstract.

60. It is a total misconception to say that, in a sense, writing   T   F
is rewriting.

Chapter 11: Public Speaking

61. A long-run benefit associated with learning to speak in   T   F
front of groups is a gain in self-confidence.

62. Extroverts tend to have a distaste for the spotlight.   T   F

63. It is correct to appreciate that a talk or speech must be a   T   F
"hit"; otherwise it is a complete "miss."

64. Moderate anxiety is motivating and will have a positive   T   F
effect on the performance associated with an oral
presentation.

65. Because they are psychological crutches, it is a bad idea   T   F
to use visual aids or handouts when making an oral
presentation.

66. It is prudent to deliver a talk with very little variation of   T   F
pitch in the voice and also to reduce the range of one's
emotional expression.

Chapter 12: Taking Exams

67. A majority of students, when interviewed or asked to   T   F
fill out questionnaires, confess to some degree of test
anxiety.

68. A multiple-choice question challenges learning by   T   F
invoking a memory retrieval process called *recall.*

69. The primary purpose of an essay question is to assess   T   F
your capacity to tie together, or make connections
among, terms, concepts, and key pieces of information.

70. Research suggests that it is almost never a good idea to   T   F
change the first choice you have marked on a given item
on a multiple-choice examination.

71. There is no distinction to be made between learning and performance.   T F

72. It is a good idea to consciously strive for a literary style when you write an essay examination.   T F

Chapter 13: Coping with Learned Helplessness

73. A feeling of helplessness is just that, a *feeling*. It is not necessarily a reflection of objective reality.   T F

74. There is no distinction of value to be made between actual helplessness and learned helplessness.   T F

75. The basic nature of the phenomenon of learned helplessness has nothing to do with generalization.   T F

76. One way to cope with learned helplessness is to focus on internal locus of control, not external locus of control.   T F

77. It is an effective coping strategy to adopt the point of view that the idea that you are helpless in certain academic situations is a *psychological construct*, a view of reality.   T F

78. Learned optimism is an idea that just doesn't work.   T F

Chapter 14: Developing an Outstanding Memory

79. Memory is best thought of as a mental faculty, an inborn power of the mind.   T F

80. Memory involves the encoding, storage, and retrieval of mental information.   T F

81. The B-complex vitamins are of no particular importance in the manufacture of key neurotransmitters associated with memory.   T F

82. A mnemonic device is of no aid to memory; it cannot give memory a boost.   T F

83. Concept learning, the least important learning that takes place in higher education, does not require insight and understanding.   T F

84. One easy way to remember a date is to relate the date to yourself.   T F

Chapter 15: Understanding Your Instructors

85. In an *I-it relationship*, the humanity of the other person is fully recognized.　　T　F

86. Anton Chekhov's story called *A Dreary Story* provides a powerful glimpse into the negative aspects of a "successful" outer career.　　T　F

87. The term *academic rank* suggests that an individual has a secure position and a certain degree of status among faculty peers.　　T　F

88. The permissive-accepting teaching style is the optimal one.　　T　F

89. If an instructor manifests an authoritarian-rejecting teaching style, you need not worry about becoming flexible and adaptable in your own behavior.　　T　F

90. If your instructor manifests a democratic-accepting teaching style, you will learn something because the course will have structure and well-defined objectives within a flexible framework.　　T　F

Chapter 16: Coping with Your Family

91. It is unlikely that members of your family will be ambivalent toward your academic goals.　　T　F

92. It is for good reason that some marriage counselors have called husbands and wives, or committed partners, intimate antagonists.　　T　F

93. You can best break out of the game called *You Always Hold Me Back* by rationalizing your academic failures in terms of the way in which your partner has failed to give you encouragement or emotional support.　　T　F

94. Children are very direct; they seldom use passive-aggressive behaviors designed to make you feel guilty about your student role.　　T　F

95. An assertiveness skill is associated with an "ideal" response between a passive one and an aggressive one.　　T　F

96. It is a good idea to talk to your partner about your academic goals in terms of vague abstractions.　　T　F

Chapter 17: Getting Ahead

97. It is necessary for you to make a choice between earning   T   F
money or properly using your intelligence and creativity.

98. The root word from which *vocation* is derived is *vocare*,   T   F
a Latin root meaning "to call."

99. Abraham Maslow asserted that one of the primitive   T   F
human motives is *self-actualization,* an inborn need to
survive and make manifest one's will to power.

100. Alfred Adler spoke of the *Creative Self,* the self in all of   T   F
us that can take charge of life, make positive decisions,
and help us reach our goals.

PART II: ANSWER KEY

1. **False.** Becoming a college student requires normal intelligence, which, by definition, most people have. (p. 2)

2. **True.** Many busy people with jobs and families take college classes on a part-time basis and have successful college careers. (p. 3)

3. **True.** There are ways to go to college on a limited income. (p. 4)

4. **False.** Although high scores on standardized examinations such as the Scholastic Assessment Test (SAT) are required for direct admission to some state universities and selective private colleges, this is not true of community colleges. (p. 5)

5. **True.** The average college graduate earns about twice as much money per year than does the average high school graduate. (p. 7)

6. **False.** Community colleges are usually fully accredited two-year institutions. (p. 15)

7. **False.** A college counselor typically has a Master's degree in counseling psychology, educational psychology, or a similar field. (p. 17)

8. **True.** The college catalog tells you what the school expects of you in the way of graduation requirements, credits, attendance, and so forth. (p. 17)

9. **True.** The idea is to *encourage* the adult who wants to go to college, not to slam a door in his or her face. (p. 18)

10. **False.** Tuition at many community colleges used to be free. Now tuition is likely to be $400 to $500 for a full-time student. (p. 19)

11. **False.** You can usually go to such institutions on a part-time basis. (p. 20)
12. **True.** For example, if you are majoring in psychology, a required general education course might be biology. (p. 24)
13. **False.** There are usually counselors and faculty members on standby who have lists of open and closed classes. (p. 26)
14. **True.** The institution *will* abide by the statements made in the catalog. (p. 28)
15. **False.** The goal of placement tests is to measure your *skill level*. (p. 28)
16. **True.** A percentile score utilizes a base of 100. (p. 29)
17. **True.** The idea of general education courses is to make you somewhat conversant with the spectrum of human knowledge. (p. 30)
18. **False.** The overall college dropout rate is discouraging. Probably no more than one-half of people who attend college ever earn a four-year degree. (p. 33)
19. **False.** The high-risk student usually has a negative self-concept as a student. (p. 35)
20. **False.** The two basic kinds of tests that are helpful are aptitude and interest tests. (p. 36)
21. **True.** The main function of an adult reentry center is to provide counseling and guidance that make returning to school *really possible*. (p. 37)
22. **True.** The money associated with scholarships and grants does not have to be repaid. The money associated with loans has to be repaid with interest. (p. 38)
23. **True.** The academic adviser is an instructor who teaches a specific subject such as history, English, biology, or accounting. (p. 39)
24. **False.** There is an enormous amount of difference between reading and studying. (p. 46)
25. **True.** Voluntary attention can be distinguished from involuntary attention. (p. 46)
26. **False.** Change of stimulation is an important factor controlling involuntary attention. (p. 47)
27. **False.** SQ3R stands for *survey, question, read, recite,* and *review*. (p. 48)

28. **True.** Studies by educational psychologists and learning theorists suggest that recitation is one of the most important steps in the SQ3R method. (p. 51)

29. **False.** It is a good idea to combine the SQ3R method with the use of flash cards. (p. 52)

30. **False.** Learning is defined as a more or less permanent change in behavior, or a behavioral tendency, as a result of experience. (p. 56)

31. **True.** The word *contiguity* means "touching" or "going together." (p. 57)

32. **False.** You can use the classical conditioning process to your advantage by arranging that the cues, or conditioned stimuli, for your study behavior be familiar, convenient ones. (p. 60)

33. **True.** Stop when you have completed the unit and give yourself a small, easily obtained reinforcer. (p. 61)

34. **True.** Insights tend to endure. We are not likely to forget them. (p. 62)

35. **False.** Because of the *learning to learn* principle, your learning tasks become easier as you progress up the academic ladder. (p. 63)

36. **True.** There is a positive side to slow learning. Information that is acquired with effort and by a slow process is generally retained for a long time. (p. 65)

37. **False.** The term *underachiever* labels the individual; it tends to categorize him or her as "a loser." The term *underachievement syndrome* suggests a cluster of signs and symptoms; it helps us pinpoint trouble areas. (p. 68)

38. **True.** *Denial of reality* is a psychological process that allows an individual to discount important facts. (p. 69)

39. **True.** A lack of identity is associated with muddled dreams and goals and a general lack of direction in life. (p. 71)

40. **False.** Poor nutrition can contribute to conditions such as an imbalance of key neurotransmitters in the brain or to hypoglycemia, both of which can have an adverse impact on motivation and behavior. (p. 73)

41. **True.** An unconscious motive can be a factor in a self-defeating pattern. (p. 73)

42. **True.** Incentives allow you to anticipate and imagine positive outcomes. (p. 77)

43. **True.** Perhaps one-half of college students suffer from math anxiety ranging in intensity from moderate to severe. (p. 80)

44. **True.** The use of concrete examples was first recommended by Maria Montessori, an Italian educator who did her major research more than 70 years ago. (p. 82)

45. **True.** It is a popular idea that some people may be left-brain dominant and others may be right-brain dominant. (p. 82)

46. **True.** A nonredundant language presents formidable barriers because it allows no latitude for mistakes. (p. 85)

47. **False.** The desensitization process is a natural learning process in which repeated exposure to a fearful stimulus robs that stimulus of its power to evoke anxiety. (p. 88)

48. **False.** The ideas contained in an inferiority complex are not necessarily true. (p. 89)

49. **False.** Time management is a voluntary process in which specific skills are used to reduce stress and increase effectiveness by budgeting time in a rational manner. (p. 92)

50. **False.** The *time-pressure syndrome* consists of a set of negative and self-defeating attitudes and behaviors. (p. 92)

51. **True.** Behaviors associated with perfectionism take up an inordinate amount of time and contribute to the time-pressure syndrome. (p. 95)

52. **True.** Make an informal list of the three or four most important things that you want to accomplish in a given day. (p. 97)

53. **True.** A schedule is, in effect, a time map; consequently it is a very helpful guide. (p. 98)

54. **False.** If you are time oriented, you will tend to watch the clock and be impatient for time to pass. (p. 100)

55. **False.** A term paper is an opportunity for you to display that you can make connections among concepts, do a little research, and express your thoughts in a clear form. (p. 103)

56. **True.** It is a good idea to set forth a paper's thesis as a formal, explicitly stated proposition early in the paper. (p. 104)

57. **False.** An encyclopedia article is a secondary source of information; it has been derived from primary ones. (p. 105)

58. **True.** The four basic stages of creative thinking can be readily applied in the actual production of a term paper. (p. 107)

59. **False.** The writing in a term paper should be clear and to the point. (p. 109)

60. **False.** It is an important point to remember that, in a sense, writing is rewriting. (p. 110)

61. **True.** Positive experiences rub off on your whole personality and tend to give you a lift. (p. 113)

62. **False.** Introverts, not extroverts, tend to have a distaste for the spotlight. (p. 114)

63. **False.** The idea that a speech is either a great success or a total failure is fallacious either-or thinking. (p. 115)

64. **True.** You don't need to get rid of *all* anxiety when you give a talk. (p. 116)

65. **False.** Even though they are psychological crutches, it is generally a good idea to use visual aids or handouts when giving an oral presentation. (p. 118)

66. **False.** A talk delivered with feeling and liveliness will go over far better with an audience than one that is overcontrolled. (p. 120)

67. **True.** If you commonly experience test anxiety, you are not alone. (p. 123)

68. **False.** A multiple-choice question challenges learning by invoking a memory retrieval process called *recognition*. (p. 124)

69. **True.** More is demanded by good essay questions than the sheer ability to remember and reproduce information. (p. 126)

70. **False.** Research suggests that if a student changes 10 or 12 answers in a 50-question multiple-choice test, about 70 percent of the changes will have a positive impact on the overall score. (p. 128)

71. **False.** Learning refers to what you actually know about a subject. Performance refers to your capacity to make that learning evident to others. (p. 129)

72. **False.** On an essay examination, you should say what you have to say as directly and as clearly as possible. (p. 131)

73. **True.** A feeling of helplessness is frequently the result of a self-defeating attitude. (p. 135)

74. **False.** Psychologists make a formal distinction between actual helplessness and learned helplessness. (p. 135)

75. **False.** Generalization is the basic psychological process involved in learned helplessness. (p. 137)

76. **True.** When a person tends to focus on internal locus of control, he or she feels in charge of life. (p. 139)

77. **True.** Once you realize that your psychological world is *built by you*—"constructed"—you can separate this world from the real, objective world. (p. 139)

78. **False.** Learned optimism is a useful concept. (p. 139)

79. **False.** Memory is best thought of as a process, a way in which information is dealt with by the mind. (p. 143)

80. **True.** In order to develop an effective memory, it is important to pay some attention to each of the three subprocesses involved in memory. (p. 143)

81. **False.** The B-complex vitamins *are* of particular importance in the manufacture of key neurotransmitters associated with memory. (p. 147)

82. **False.** A mnemonic device is an aid to memory, something that gives memory a boost. (p. 149)

83. **False.** Concept learning, the most important learning that takes place in higher education, requires insight and understanding. (p. 150)

84. **True.** If you will subtract a date to be remembered from your own birthdate, this will make the date to be remembered more meaningful. (p. 153)

85. **False.** In an *I-thou relationship,* not an *I-it relationship,* the humanity of another person is fully recognized. (p. 157)

86. **True.** Chekov's story provides a sober glimpse into the human side of a professor's life. (p. 158)

87. **True.** Academic rank in most colleges is formal, and the individual in question has a rank of assistant professor, associate professor, or full professor. (p. 159)

88. **False.** The democratic-accepting style is the optimal one. (p. 163)

89. **False.** If an instructor manifests an authoritarian-rejecting style, you must become as flexible and adaptable as possible. (p. 164)

90. **True.** If an instructor manifests a democratic-accepting style, do your part and meet the instructor halfway, and you can expect to succeed in the course. (p. 166)

91. **False.** It is likely that members of your family will be ambivalent, feeling both positive and negative attitudes toward your student role. (p. 168)

92. **True.** Husbands and wives, or committed partners, often oppose each other in important ways. (p. 170)

93. **False.** You can best break out of the game called *You Always Hold Me Back* by deciding that you *are not* going to set up a rationalization for failure by self-indulgently blaming your partner. (p. 171)

94. **False.** Children may try to make you feel guilty with passive-aggressive strategies because they lack the self-confidence or the clarity of perception required to confront you directly, negotiate, and reason logically. (p. 172)

95. **True.** An assertive response lets you stand up for your rights in a rational, firm manner. (p. 173)

96. **False.** Talk to your partner about your academic goals in concrete terms, not vague abstractions. (p. 174)

97. **False.** Either-or thinking about life's pathways is logically fallacious. (p. 178)

98. **True.** Your "true vocation" is, in brief, what you are "meant to do" with your life. (p. 178)

99. **False.** Abraham Maslow asserted that one of the highest human motives is *self-actualization*, an inborn need to make the most of our talents and potentialities. (p. 179)

100. **True.** The discovery of your own *Creative Self* can help you to escape from learned helplessness and other negative factors that may act as barriers to achievement. (p. 181)

PART III: SCORING GUIDE

Each correct answer is worth one point. Use this scoring guide:

> 91–100 = Excellent
> 81–90 = Good
> 71–80 = Fair
> 61–70 = Barely passing
> 51–60 = Failure

If you are disappointed with your score, maintain a positive attitude. Review in the Answer Key the brief explanations associated with the questions you missed. If you need a more complete explanation for a given item, use the page reference provided to quickly look up essential material. An *active* review of your errors will help you fill in your knowledge gaps. Wait a few days and take the examination a second time.

If you received a score that pleased you, I congratulate you. You have acquired the kind of information and understanding that will help you become an effective college student.

ABOUT THE AUTHOR

Frank J. Bruno, Ph.D., is Professor of Psychology at San Bernadino Valley College in California. He has given guidance to hundreds of adults who either are thinking of going to college or are already enrolled. He is the author of eleven prior books. These include *The Story of Psychology, Think Yourself Thin, Behavior and Life, Adjustment and Personal Growth, Dictionary of Key Words in Psychology, The Family Mental Health Encyclopedia, The Family Encyclopedia of Child Psychology and Development,* and *Psychological Symptoms.*